A Time to Heal

Also by Timmen L. Cermak, M.D.:

A Primer for Adult Children of Alcoholics
Diagnosing and Treating Codependency:
A Guide for Professionals
Evaluating and Treating Adult Children of Alcoholics:
A Guide for Professionals (in press)

A
Time
to
Heal

The Road to Recovery for Adult Children of Alcoholics

Timmen L. Cermak, M.D.

JEREMY P. TARCHER, INC.
Los Angeles
Distributed by St. Martin's Press
New York

Library of Congress Cataloging in Publication Data

Cermak, Timmen L.
    A time to heal: the road to recovery for adult children of alcoholics /
by Timmen L. Cermak.
      p.   cm.
    Bibliography.
    Includes index.
    ISBN 0-87477-454-3
    1. Adult children of alcoholics—United States. I. Title.
HV5132.C45 1988
362.8'2—dc19   87-29127
                                              CIP

JEREMY P. TARCHER, INC.
9110 Sunset Blvd.
Los Angeles, CA 90069

Design by Rosa Schuth

Manufactured in the United States of America
10 9 8 7 6 5 4 3 2 1

First Edition

This book is dedicated to Lois, Rhita, George, Laird, Cyndie, Mary, and Elizabeth.

Everything Has Its Time

To everything there is a season,
  A time for every purpose under heaven:

A time to be born,
  And a time to die;
A time to plant,
  And a time to pluck what is planted;
A time to kill,
  And a time to heal;
A time to break down,
  And a time to build up;
A time to weep,
  And a time to laugh;
A time to mourn,
  And a time to dance;
A time to cast away stones,
  And a time to gather stones;
A time to embrace,
  And a time to refrain from embracing;
A time to gain
  And a time to lose;
A time to keep,
  And a time to throw away;
A time to tear,
  And a time to sew;
A time to keep silence,
  And a time to speak;
A time to love,
  And a time to hate;
A time of war,
  And a time of peace.

Ecclesiastes, Chapter 3, Verses 1–8

Contents

Acknowledgments

I continue to appreciate the training in alcoholism and children of alcoholics that I received from Dr. Stephanie Brown. Her ability to bridge the gap between traditional psychotherapy and the chemical-dependence field remains an inspiration.

The faith and honesty of countless adult children of alcoholics who have been in therapy with me has contributed immensely to the writing of this book. I trust that I have understood your stories accurately and have altered them sufficiently to protect everyone's identity. In many instances, two or more stories have been combined to concentrate their emotional truth.

Colleagues with whom I have shared the pleasure of founding the National Association for Children of Alcoholics have left indelible impressions on my work. It is impossible to sort out which influences have come from each. I thank and respect you all.

The staff at Genesis (our San Francisco–based center for treating adult children of alcoholics and codependents) have been a constant source of stimulation and understanding. Their input permeates this book.

Finally, I am grateful for the invaluable comments on early drafts from Marilyn Meshak, Peter Beren, Mary Brand Cermak (my colleague and wife), and Jeremy Tarcher. You have all helped me throw out that which was confusing and unclear by gently emphasizing what was done well. Without your sensitivity, I might still be defending mistakes made in the first draft. The editorial work by Hank Stine consistently proved to be of critical value to organizing and smoothing out the manuscript, and Mary Nadler's final editing gave the book a polish it would not otherwise have had.

Author's Note

All personal stories contained in *A Time to Heal* are emotionally accurate, but the factual information has been modified to protect identities. Each story stems from the lives of people I have seen in therapy, and never from the author's imagination. I am deeply indebted to these people for all they have taught me.

Introduction: Huck and I

I was fascinated by Huckleberry Finn from the moment I met him through Mark Twain's writing. To all appearances, my own life was quite different from his. Huck lived during a time of feuds and flimflam men in rough-and-ready pre–Civil War America. I attended an average school in Ohio during the 1950s, studied diligently, and had never met a real criminal. Huck took off on his own and rafted the wild Mississippi River. I rode my bike to school occasionally. Huck's mother was dead, and his father beat the tar out of him. My parents got divorced when I was thirteen, but I was never left without a roof over my head.

On the surface, Huck's life and mine were worlds apart. So why have I always responded to him as though he were a twin brother? When I reread Twain's book as an adult, I finally understood the bond. My fascination and sense of kinship with Huck made complete sense at last: we are both children of alcoholic fathers.

The Adventures of Huckleberry Finn leaves no doubt about Mr. Finn's alcoholism. "Every time he got money he got drunk; and every time he got drunk he raised Cain around town; and every time he raised Cain he got jailed." He drank so much that his face was drained of color and white—"not like another man's white, but a white to make a body sick, a white to make a body's flesh crawl." He drank until he hallucinated and lost all memory. In one frightening episode, Huck witnessed his father screaming about imaginary snakes

1

crawling up his legs and biting him on the neck. Later that
night, Huck relates, "He chased me round and round the
place with a clasp-knife, calling me the Angel of Death and
saying he would kill me."

Huck's father was a violent man who beat Huck until the
boy was covered with welts. He was a bitter man who blamed
all of his misfortune on others. He was a spiteful man who
resented Huck's "school learning"; he vowed to take Huck
down a peg for putting on airs and tore up an award his son
had received from school. He was a public disgrace, the
acknowledged town drunk. When a new judge in town naively
took Mr. Finn into his home to reform him, Huck's father
promptly stole enough money to get drunk, rolled off the
porch roof, broke his arm in two places, and almost froze to
death before sunup. Today, we recognize Mr. Finn as a very
sick man. The disease of alcoholism ruined his life and led
him to a premature death.

In his drunken view of the world, Mr. Finn saw Huck
as his personal possession. He terrorized Huck to get drinking money (which Huck quickly gave him in order to avoid
getting a beating). Whenever Huck showed any independence, his father literally held him hostage. At times he would
not let Huck out of his sight for days; at other times he would
simply take off, leaving the boy locked up in their remote
cabin. Huck had no right to exist, except to make his father's
life easier. When the widow who had cared for Huck during
his father's yearlong absence asked to have protective custody
of him, the courts refused to interfere. The judge said that he
did not want to separate families if he could avoid it.

Huckleberry Finn was the child of an alcoholic (CoA),
and this experience profoundly affected his life. Beneath his
bravado was fear. Under his bubbling enthusiasm was a boy
who knew enough depression and loneliness to almost wish
for death at times. He suffered from guilt far out of proportion
to anything he had done, and he felt responsible for others'
misfortune. Whenever his life lacked drama, Huck would

become bored and would long for change of any kind. He lived behind a facade of fabrication so pervasive that telling the truth felt strange. His strategy for getting through life was to escape, to keep out of quarrels, to let other people have their own way, and to keep the roots of commitment to anyone or anything from sinking too deeply. Throughout it all, he wrestled with his own sense of self-worth.

There is a lot of Huckleberry Finn in every child of an alcoholic. You may recognize the kinship you feel with him without understanding its source. His experience is a mirror in which you may see many of your hopes and fears reflected. You may see your own deep sense of being an outsider, your own unrelenting drive to survive. And you may see yourself on the run, trying to get away from a past that can never be left far enough behind.

By and large, the effects of being raised by an alcoholic parent have not changed much in the last hundred years. In the beginning of the book, Huck found himself in a dilemma, bouncing back and forth between two intolerable situations. Whenever he spent time with the widow as his guardian, life became boring. He attended school, was taught religion, took daily baths, and had to stop cussing and smoking his pipe. Life seemed empty without the drama of surviving his father's drunken binges and the adventure of fending for himself when his Pap disappeared for days at a time. On the other hand, whenever he fled the widow, Huck became a hostage to his father's beatings and insanity.

On the terrifying night when his drunken father chased him around the cabin with a knife, Huck grabbed a rifle off the wall and held him at bay until he finally passed out from the alcohol. Sleep eventually overtook Huck as well. The next morning, he was awakened by his father, who, with no memory of the night before, demanded to know why Huck was sleeping crouched by the door with the gun across his knees. Huck immediately judged that it was best not to tell the truth. "Somebody tried to get in, so I was laying for him," he said.

Today, such creativity in a person's survival instincts is called street sense. In the middle of the last century it was called river sense. Huck instinctively understood that his father had no memory of what had happened the previous night (such episodes are called alcohol-induced memory lapses, or blackouts). He therefore took the opportunity to make up a different version of reality, one that felt safer than the truth.

Most people living with an out-of-control alcoholic learn not to make unnecessary waves. Reality becomes what the alcoholic is willing to accept as reality. Huck's response to a world that was out of his control and that cared little about who he was as an individual symbolizes the response of most CoAs.

Freedom through escape made the most sense to Huck, and the only way he felt able to escape was by staging his own death. When his father was away, Huck smashed down the door of their cabin with an axe and rummaged around for provisions. Then Huck shot a wild pig and smeared its blood on his bedcovers and on the axe. He pulled out some of his own hairs, stuck them to the axe's blade, and tossed the axe into the corner as evidence of his murder. Finally, he conspicuously dragged the pig's body down to the water's edge, leaving "evidence" that his own body had been tossed into the river. Then he disappeared on his adventures down the Mississippi.

Huck's trip down the Mississippi River serves as a metaphor for the journey made by children of alcoholics as they attempt to leave home and make lives of their own. This journey is largely motivated by the dream of escape, and it is all too frequently bought at the price of cooperating with one's own death—emotional, spiritual, or even physical.

Huck's creed for life is expressed in his thoughts on how to have a successful raft trip. He felt that there must be no conflict; his way of dealing with negative feelings was to say nothing, never to let on, to keep things to himself. "It's the best way; then you don't have no quarrels, and don't get into no trouble." He tells us, "If I never learnt nothing else out of Pap, I learnt that the best way to get along with his kind of people is to let them have their own way."

When two swindlers hitched a ride on his raft, Huck knew they "warn't no kings nor dukes at all, but just low-down humbugs and frauds." But if they wanted Huck to call them kings and dukes, then he had no objections, " 'long as it would keep peace in the family."

Being a CoA, Huck understood that the perfect way to disguise yourself is to let other people see in you whatever they want to see. Up against uncontrollable forces, Huck learned to take on a chameleonlike quality. No matter whom he fell in with, he could take on their characteristics or mold himself to get what he needed from them. In the course of his adventures, Huck was befriended by a whole gallery of characters, including feuding Southern aristocrats and confidence men. At one point, Tom Sawyer's Aunt Sally mistook Huck for Tom, who was expected to arrive momentarily for a summer vacation. Huck, in need of a good meal, played the part perfectly before he even knew who the woman thought he was. When she introduced him to his "cousins" as Tom Sawyer, Huck was stunned: "It was like being born again, I was so glad to find out who I was." From that point on, he simply became Tom Sawyer.

Children of alcoholics tend to have the chameleon nature that Huck so often showed. While this trait can be charming and useful, it can also become such a habit that it turns into a prison from which a person's real identity never fully emerges.

Being an underdog throughout his life, Huck had sympathy for underdogs everywhere. He befriended a runaway slave and repeatedly risked his own safety to keep his friend free. At another point, he put himself in great danger to foil a plot to swindle three newly orphaned girls out of their inheritance, cleverly leaving the con men to argue between themselves over which one was to blame for losing the money.

6 A TIME TO HEAL

Huck's heart softened each time he saw someone down on his luck. He understood from his own experience how easily this could happen.

Huck's kindheartedness also stems to some degree from the exaggerated guilt experienced by so many adult children of alcoholics (ACAs). He frequently felt guilty for things, even when he knew he had done nothing to cause the misfortune. "But that's always the way; it don't make no difference whether you do right or wrong, a person's conscience ain't got no sense, and it just goes for him *anyway*." When Huck was caught in the middle of two feuding families and saw one of the boys get shot, he knew he could not go near that family's house again, "because I reckoned I was to blame, somehow."

Toward the end of the book, Huck learned that his father had died. Huck no longer had any reason to keep on running and could safely return to Hannibal. What happens in the book's last half-page tells us a lot about Huckleberry Finn.

Running had become a way of life. Rather than settling down to a relatively normal life and allowing himself to be adopted by Tom Sawyer's aunt, Huck said that he had heard of some excitement up in Indian country (probably Oklahoma), and he reckoned he would light out for there in search of further adventure. Although this warms the heart, and the reader roots for Huck to remain forever a boy in search of excitement, it also represents another way in which Huck had been molded by his experience of growing up with an alcoholic parent. It was not only the thirst for freedom that burned brightly in Huck's breast; fear also propelled him to seek escape as a way of life.

At the end of the book, Huck's strategies all seem to be working, but Huck is still a child. It is unlikely that his way of accommodating to life's problems provided a firm foundation for a full, rich, and satisfying adult life or for successful intimate relationships. For Huck, as for so many millions of other CoAs, running had become the goal. He *had* to keep running, if he was to feel safe. But, as with so many ACAs, Huck would certainly have run out of gas at some point and had to face what it was he had been running from all those years. He would have discovered that he had begun by running from his father but had ended up running from himself. Living in a survival mode is one of the major characteristics of ACAs.

The final two paragraphs of the book also illustrate how distanced Huck had become from some of his emotions. On hearing of his father's death he had absolutely no reaction. Had he come to have no feelings whatsoever for his father? More likely, he was not aware of what his feelings were. One is left to wonder how many years it would be before Huck would finally allow himself to react to having lost his father.

In an interesting deviation from Mark Twain's book, a Public Broadcasting System movie of *Huckleberry Finn* chose to have Huck learn of his father's death much earlier in the story. The PBS version had Huck immediately deny that his father had ever treated him badly. Huck also concluded that he might have somehow been responsible for his father's death. Although these reactions were not contained in the original book, they certainly depict how a child of an alcoholic might respond.

If Huck was ever to heal the wounds suffered at his father's hands, it would have been through the rigid honesty he possessed. During his deepest crisis of the spirit, he was confronted with his tendency to try to escape the consequences of his misdeeds by keeping them hidden. He tried to excuse himself for this by saying that he had been brought up to be wicked, but he recognized that he could have gone to church and set this right. He knelt to pray, but no words would come. It was then that he realized his deepest flaw. He had been playing double, trying to pray for something when he knew deep down it was a lie. Huck discovered that "you can't pray a lie." It was this willingness to see his own denial (which I will discuss at length in chapter 2) that gives me the most hope that Huck may eventually have been able to stop running.

If Huck never found a way to stop running, it would have been because he cooperated with his own death. The elaborate staging of his own murder symbolizes the way in which CoAs often obtain an element of freedom in their lives by accepting their own unimportance. By going into hiding, by being less than what they normally would be, by opting out of the reality they have been placed in, CoAs obtain some sense of control over lives that are otherwise taken over by others and thrown into chaos.

Mark Twain gave us no idea of what eventually became of Huckleberry Finn. I prefer to imagine that he traveled with the Buffalo Bill Wild West Show or joined the Yukon gold rush. But I have nightmares of his lying drunk and destitute in a back alley of Hannibal, Missouri, still a loner, compulsively seeking excitement until the end. Huck did say, "I'd druther been bit with a snake than Pap's whiskey"—but what CoA hasn't made such a statement?

There are lessons of universal value to be learned from the struggles of CoAs. Above all is the lesson that healing begins with honesty. Huck Finn demonstrated such honesty when he had the integrity to admit that he was trying to pray a lie; he knew his deepest flaw was that he played double with life. This flaw can only be dissolved by making the discipline of recovery a part of daily life. *A Time to Heal* will prepare you to understand this discipline, will outline it for you, and will give you a vision of the direction in which it can take you.

Part 1

The Road Ahead

This book carries the promise of hope. It is the hope that after the cold and darkness of winter comes another season—the time to heal.

The kind of healing that reaches deeply into your spirit cannot be hurried. Neither can it be passively awaited. The soil within must be tilled. Seeds must be planted and watered. Weeds must be pulled. All this work takes commitment to yourself and to the future.

Part 1 looks at the road to recovery that lies ahead of you. The first chapter describes the bountiful harvest that can be anticipated. Without the hope for such a harvest, there is little reason to embark on the difficult journey. Chapter 2 outlines the first steps that must be taken in order for the rest of the journey to become possible. These first steps involve pulling down the wall of denial you've erected as protection— from your feelings, from memories of the past, and from being hurt again. It is only after your denial has been dismantled that you can get an accurate view of the road you've already traveled. And it is only when you clearly see the road ahead of you, as well as the road behind, that it becomes possible to begin enjoying the journey itself.

1.

~~~~~~~~~~~~~~~~~~~~~~~~~~~~~~~~~~

A Time to Heal:
The Promise of Hope

It was a long and often arduous journey for me to come to an understanding that the bond I feel with Huckleberry Finn stems from the fact that we are both children of alcoholics. Many of the people surrounding me when I was a child had an opportunity to help me begin the journey to this understanding, but each kept silent. No family member, relative, or neighbor ever spoke a word to me about my father's alcoholism until several years after my parents had divorced.

Such silence is not uncommon. Perhaps the majority of CoAs are "protected" from the truth by friends and family who believe that it only makes things worse to talk about a parent's alcoholism. Or they are too embarrassed to talk to the child about it. Or they have not yet acknowledged the alcoholism themselves. The reasons for silence are as numerous and complicated as the people contributing to it. Whatever the reasons, such silence did not protect me. It only made it more difficult for me to discover one of the most important realities of my life—my father's disease of alcoholism.

Our family physician had ample opportunity to break the silence for me, and ample cause to believe that I was in need of knowing the truth. There is no doubt that he knew of my father's alcoholism. My mother had gone to him for advice, and he had told her that it would kill my father if she left him. I was taken to this doctor when I was six for stress-related intestinal cramps. The doctor did nothing to help me acknowledge the tension under which I was living. Instead, he suggested that I wear my belt looser.

Our minister never said anything to me about the trouble in my family, although he made monthly visits because of the situation. None of the neighbors spoke to me of the real problems in my home. None of my relatives, who were painfully aware of my father's drinking, spoke to me about it. The silence was complete.

Although all these people were essentially well meaning, each of them shrank from the knowledge that children have strong feelings and need to be given invitations to verbalize them. They were all in denial, to one degree or another. As the next chapter will explore, being in denial does not always mean that you are unaware of the alcoholism. Sometimes it means that you choose to remain unaware of how much someone else's alcoholism is affecting you and other family members. Other times it means that you are not willing to acknowledge the intensity of feelings that children are bound to have whenever the bond between them and their parents is threatened, as it invariably is when a parent is alcoholic.

When I decided on a career in psychiatry, I knew it meant the beginning of a trip back through my childhood. But I never realized that it would mean revisiting painful childhood memories of my father's alcoholism, or that it would eventually lead to a career of treating other adults who had grown up in alcoholic homes. I was in denial about how much my father's disease had been the workbench upon which my own personality was molded. I thought I had escaped being affected.

I could have lived the rest of my life without coming to realistic terms with the disease of alcoholism and how it had affected my family and my very personality. Many people do. I don't know if I ever would have developed more awareness had I been left to my own devices. Fortunately, we are never left entirely on our own. I soon stumbled—or was guided by an invisible hand—into contact with a person who stimulated and nurtured new awareness in me.

During my training in psychiatry at Stanford University Medical Center, I was required to attend a seminar on alcoholism taught by Stephanie Brown, Ph.D. Beyond Dr. Brown's animated and skillful style of lecturing, the course held no particular interest for me during the first five weeks. Little did I know the impact it was about to have.

The topic in the sixth week was "Children of Alcoholics." During the lecture I felt myself riveted by Dr. Brown's words. A sense of strangeness filled my head as I recognized that she was describing my day-to-day experiences as a child with uncanny accuracy. It was as though I had had a recurring dream throughout my life that I had never told to another person, and then, one day I found myself in a room where a woman was standing up in front of everyone, relating my dream in such detail that she was reminding me of aspects of it that even I had forgotten. I was stunned. Not even my individual therapist, whom I had seen for more than a year, could have outlined my inner sense of reality as clearly as Stephanie Brown was doing.

Two things resulted from that lecture. First, my self-image underwent a sudden revision. Until then I had always assumed that my underlying beliefs about the world, my attitudes about life, and my unresolved emotional ties to the past were unique to me. Suddenly I learned that they were all predictable reactions to the experiences of most children who grow up in alcoholic homes. My distorted views were understandable and did not rise from within my essential character. Instead, they were reactions to a stressful environment.

Second, I knew that I had to explore further what this new information might mean to me personally. My journey had begun in earnest.

AN OVERVIEW OF THE JOURNEY

My purpose in writing *A Time to Heal* is to communicate the understanding and hope that this journey has taught me, both personally and professionally. It has taught me that real healing begins only when we are willing to make the past real. Making the past real means not only recalling events that have been buried in time but also resurrecting the feelings we had during those events and taking their full measure. This means looking directly at the wounds alcoholic families inflict on developing children. It is important that we make contact again with the child we were in order to finally give that child validation for the feelings he or she was having. Only by giving the child within us a voice, even after all these years, can we begin to believe at a deep level that we are not bad or crazy ourselves.

Each journey has a first step. That first step is often the most difficult one of all, because taking it is an acknowledgment of the need to make the whole journey—before there is any guarantee that the journey is worth the effort or can ever be completed. This act of faith is so scary that people tend to deny that the journey is really necessary. "After all," you may say to yourself, "it isn't too bad where I am now." Sometimes this acceptance of our current life, complete with all its flaws, is the sign of great maturity. Other times it means we are blind to the problems affecting us. Ignorance may not be bliss, but at least it's familiar.

The tendency to deal with our problems by denying their existence or their effect on us is so prevalent among alcoholics and their families that it must be looked at directly (chapter 2) before the journey has any chance of being started. Adult children of alcoholics are masters at not listening to the child's voice within, because they deny that a child even exists there. Or they deny that the child needs to be heard. Until this denial is dismantled, your present psychological state will remain unchanged.

Alcoholic homes are not normal homes. Once your denial diminishes, you can begin to look more realistically at what it was like to be a kid in your family. Children of alcoholics often complain of not knowing what "normal" is because they have had no experience with healthy role models. I have heard ACAs tell of walking around their neighborhoods as children and looking in windows of other houses to see how normal families lived. It is only after they have learned the characteristics of healthy functioning that they can see the destructive dynamics that ruled their families (chapter 3).

Growing up in the highly stressful environment of an alcoholic family creates wounds that often go underground. When they emerge later in life, it isn't easy to connect these wounds with their real source.

Whether the stress of a parent's alcoholism is obvious or subtle, it leaves its mark. These wounds cause many ACAs to unintentionally diminish the quality of their lives because they cannot allow themselves to trust the world. People learn by their experiences, and the experiences of many CoAs have taught them that trusting the world is not wise. The world of their childhood changed too often, too abruptly, and too painfully to engender trust.

Many of the personality characteristics of ACAs stem from their having been locked in a survival mode. Strategies designed for coping with chaos and catastrophe have been put on automatic pilot, even when they are no longer needed. The concept of post-traumatic stress disorder, which is most often associated with the problems experienced by many Vietnam veterans after returning home from the trauma of combat, helps us understand the CoA's wounds. The loss of trust in both the world and in themselves, along with the accompanying losses of spontaneity and of the ability to relax, are wounds that can last a lifetime (chapter 4).

My journey has taught me that alcoholic families not only inflict wounds on children but also teach potentially dangerous ways of caring for the wounds—which can com-

pound the original problem. For CoAs, this poor care takes
the form of learning the same ineffective, even self-destructive, strategies for coping with life's problems as those used
by alcoholics. The word *codependent* is used to describe any
family member who deals with the alcoholic's and family's
problems primarily by denying them. Most alcoholic families
are highly codependent (chapter 5).

Although many of the wounds affecting ACAs lie deep
in the past, there are invariably ways in which each of us
keeps the wounds festering. The painful events that happened
in the past can never be changed. What *can* be changed is the
perpetuation of the pain into the present (chapter 6). Understanding how we can alter our current behavior in order to
resolve many old wounds opens up the possibility of deep and
gratifying recovery. The threshold of healing has been
reached.

My journey has now brought me to a place of great hope.
It has shown me that a path toward healing and recovery
exists for CoAs (chapters 7, 8, and 9). Ironically, this path was
first charted by people recovering from alcoholism. Since
CoAs learn most of their attitudes toward themselves and the
world from alcoholics, it should not be surprising that the
path leading to recovery for both are quite similar. This path
is becoming well-worn and well-populated these days.

Each individual ACA is still responsible for taking his
or her own steps. No one can walk for you. But knowing that
you are no longer alone in your journey makes the path much
less difficult. Others have gone before and freely share their
experience with fellow travelers, pointing the way to the
world you'll live in once you have made a commitment to your
recovery.

Finally, understanding the effects of growing up in an
alcoholic home has taught me much about the very nature of
being human. There is comfort in this. It counteracts the
conviction among ACAs that their experience is so different
that it sets them apart from the rest of the human race. Quite

the opposite is true. Through the extremes of our experiences, we can catch a clearer glimpse of the human condition itself. In the lessons that can be learned from the lives of CoAs— lessons that are important to all children—we touch upon what is universal.

One facet of the human condition that is thrown into stark relief by the experiences of ACAs is the tendency of children to regard their parents as perfect. Greater maturation eventually robs us of this illusion. In its place must come the realities of who our parents are as specific, concrete individuals. In return for relinquishing our illusions, we create the possibility that we will feel more empathy for our parents as well as for ourselves.

All people are faced with the difficult tasks of separating their identities from those of their parents, of discarding their childhood illusions of the perfect parents, and of developing empathy for both themselves and for their parents as real people. Children of alcoholics tend to have more than the usual amount of difficulty with these tasks. By understanding what creates these difficulties, we gain valuable insights into basic human nature. We are reminded that children are living, learning, absorbing creatures. Children have an absolute need to be touched by other people, both physically and emotionally. They develop a sense of who they are only by being in relationships with others. If they are ever to feel good about themselves, children must be respected and esteemed. When they are ignored, they feel unimportant. When they are shamed or embarrassed, they feel unworthy. And when they are degraded, they feel self-hatred. The demons that grow in a parent's garden will find ways of taking root, in one disguise or another, in their child's garden as well.

We all emerge from childhood with wounds. By understanding the process of healing among ACAs, we begin to recognize that the path of recovery has universal application. The steps that ACAs must take to free themselves from being hostages to the past are steps that others can also use to help free themselves from the damage done to them in the past. These steps point toward a vision of health, freedom, and balance for all who are willing to follow them.

INCLUDING YOURSELF IN THE JOURNEY

With the time to heal comes a time to belong. An increasing number of ACAs are coming to terms with the pain, fear, and chaos of the past and entering into recovery. You, too, can become a part of the community they are creating. If what you are about to read does nothing more than end your isolation, the seeds of recovery will have been planted.

Even though you may have felt alone much of your life, you are a member of one of the largest groups in this country. You have 28 million brothers and sisters. One of every eight Americans is the child of an alcoholic. If we all stood shoulder to shoulder, we would form an unbroken line from New York, to Seattle, to Los Angeles, to Atlanta, and back to New York.

Adult children of alcoholics come from all walks of life. Many are college graduates and have very successful careers; others are unemployed, homeless, or in jail. A great number are themselves alcoholic or addicted to other drugs. Whatever their present circumstances, you share a common bond with all other ACAs. This bond is forged out of having had the same experiences of fearing, loving, needing, and hating an alcoholic parent with whom you could find no peace, and yet who occupied a position at the center of your life. If you want to experience that bond, look for it in the eyes of other ACAs when you talk about your childhood. They, too, have experienced the depths of pain you have known.

Increasingly, the common bond is also being felt among ACAs who are entering recovery, sharing their experiences, and discovering a new sense of freedom from the past. The courage and discipline to acknowledge the past is called recovery. Recovery tills the soil within, preparing the ground for the seeds of healing to fall, to grow, and to blossom. Acknowledging that you are a CoA is the beginning of tilling the soil within. Without this acknowledgment, the seeds of healing are not likely to take root.

The primary reason for looking at how an alcoholic parent affected you is that such honesty is a step in your healing. As an ACA, there are good reasons for being the person you are. The compromises you have made in life, beginning with those made in living with an alcoholic parent, have seemed successful for so long that they have faded into the background of your awareness. But each compromise tightened the reins on the possibilities in your life. While you may believe you are ✓ living a full and rich life, in actuality you could be settling for mere survival. Recovering ACAs are coming to believe that there is more to life than mere survival.

This acknowledgment is difficult because it contradicts the habit of ignoring or denying problems, a habit you learned directly from your parents. But if you can take an honest look at yourself, you may be surprised to recognize that your life fits one of the common patterns seen among ACAs.

Common ACA Patterns

- Hard-driving; workaholic; always preoccupied by projects and things that "have to be done"; rarely satisfied with accomplishments; in denial of feelings; relationships take a back seat.
- Defensive; fearful of closeness to others; play cards close to the vest; unable to deal honestly on an emotional level; longing for relationships; chronic anger.
- Overwhelmed by feelings; buffeted by emotional storms; desperately trying to get other people to behave properly; often unable to work effectively.

- Alcohol and drug addiction.
- Depressed, with a chronic sense of emptiness within; lacking a sense of direction in life; apathy; low self-esteem; may be self-destructive.
- Confused sense of identity; unable to separate from family; always taking on the characteristics of others.
- Victim identity; constant sense of being attacked, misunderstood, ignored, and betrayed—all of which (in the ACA's eyes) justifies an angry, demanding attitude toward others.
- Martyr identity; long-suffering; unwilling to take care of oneself; constantly excusing the faults of others; willingness to submit oneself to painful situations for others' sake.
- Generous, helpful, and thoughtful—to a fault.
- Constantly searching for answers, rules, and guidelines for finding happiness and social/emotional success. Unwillingness to trust own instincts. Believing there ought to be a "right way."

✓   For some CoAs, there *was* a period of time when the family was not held hostage to a parent's drinking. For these people there is an image available of a trustworthy world that can be recalled and used as a guide to a life beyond mere survival. Others have no such model of the world. These CoAs were born into families where alcoholism was already at its peak. As infants, they were immediately awash in the chaos and insanity; things only got worse from that point on. There is no experience of a life that can be radically better. For these people, a healthier way of life has to be built from the ground up. If you are such a person, you may wonder how you can "recover" a sense of self you never had.

Life is not fair. Some of us *do* have further to travel than others. However, the steps are the same in all cases. The *integrity* with which we approach this journey is ultimately what recovery is all about. Progress, not perfection, is the purpose of our journey.

The first step toward your recovery is an acknowledgment of your parent's alcoholism. Until you are willing to explore what being the adult child of an alcoholic means, including all the feelings this raises, you are left without knowing what it is you have to recover from. Without a diagnosis of the problem, no healing is possible.

Like most ACAs, you probably have a million excuses for not acknowledging how your parent's drinking has affected you. Your life is already sufficiently stressful; now is not a good time to add further strain. Or your life is going well right now; why rock the boat? Or your parent's drinking was not *that* bad. Or the holidays are almost here; why spoil everything? Or it's Friday, or Saturday, or Sunday . . .

The reasons are endless. The truth is that all these reasons are good ones; however, they are exactly the same reasons used by alcoholics to justify not looking more realistically at their drinking.

You may have been trying so long, so desperately, and so unsuccessfully to "fix" yourself that any talk about real healing seems like too much to hope for. You may have spent years bending over backward to make a failing marriage work. You may have sacrificed a lifetime being a perfect employee without ever having had your loyalty rewarded. You may have bought every self-help book published for the past ten years and attended every imaginable personal-growth workshop without gaining anything but confusion and a feeling that there is something deeply wrong with you. You may have hidden your own feelings for so long to avoid conflict with others that now you are constantly unsure of what you *are* feeling. None of these efforts to make your life work has brought you anything but temporary relief, and you may have long ago given up hope.

The questions that ACAs ask poignantly reveal their

deep doubt that anything significant in their lives can ever change: "Why should I force myself to try one more self-help strategy, when all I've ever done is force myself into one mold after another without changing any of the underlying problems?" "Why should I set myself up to be disappointed again by believing that I can really change?" "How can I ever make up for what I never got as a child?" And later on, during the early stages of recovery: "Now that I know all this about myself and my childhood, why don't I feel any better? Why don't I change?"

The experience of recovering ACAs makes it abundantly clear that healing and growth remain possibilities throughout our lives. Our minds possess a deep capacity for healing, just as our bodies have mechanisms for healing cuts and wounds. Most of us have heard stories of alcoholics who came within inches of death, found recovery at the last moment, and today are living normal and happy lives through Twelve-Step and other programs. Many of these recovering alcoholics are themselves ACAs. The steps they took are those that can lead to your recovery as well. Never give up hope on anyone, especially yourself. Healing has a habit of coming at the unlikeliest of times—just when we have given up trying to force it to arrive.

Change *is* possible. I have seen many "impossible cases" find real healing, and I know that internal freedom and greater self-acceptance can be a reality.

- There was Betty, a thirty-five-year-old nurse with a long history of depressions following dramatic love affairs with unavailable men. When she did fall in love with someone who was eager to marry her, Betty successfully faced her own terror of such a commitment and is presently planning her wedding.
- Bob, forty-five, took the risk of confronting his wife with her alcoholism after having lived with it in silent suffering for half his life. As a result,

his wife decreased her drinking significantly, and Bob's relationship with their children suddenly became much warmer and more honest.

- Mark was a young executive who developed ulcers less than a year after graduating from business school. After he learned how to keep his work from overwhelming his personal life, Mark's work performance improved as well, and he went from having probationary status to receiving a major promotion.
- Andy, fifty, had never spoken about his father's alcoholism until his father was on his deathbed. When Andy finally broached the subject, he was stunned when his father acknowledged the truth and asked his forgiveness.
- There was Sarah, a twenty-two-year-old woman who no longer believed that she must ignore her father's dementia in order to show that she loved him.
- Ron, a thirty-two-year-old teacher, who learned that he no longer needed to base his self-worth on the ability to keep from crying about his father's drunken suicide.
- And there was Yvonne, who decided to allow long-suppressed memories of incest to rise into awareness rather than trying to make her life more manageable by ignoring them.

I have seen a time to heal come into many lives—and I know that real healing is possible for you.

A CHANGE IN ATTITUDE: THE JOURNEY INWARD

The most difficult aspect of recovery for many is that its essence lies in a change of attitude. As an ACA, you might respond to this by saying, "Fine, tell me what attitudes I'm supposed to have, and I'll make myself have them." This would never work. The first attitude we must change in order to recover involves how we go about trying to change our attitudes! The attitudes that promote healing can never be changed by force of will. In fact, the very strategy of trying to force oneself into a different mold hinders recovery. The attitude of recovery must be invited to happen. We can only ✓ till the soil within and pray for the willingness to change.

Recovery requires an acceptance of the paradox that although our attitudes must change, we have no direct control over them. Simply forcing ourselves to behave in new ways is no guarantee that changes in attitude will follow.

Jane is a thirty-three-year-old mother and fashion designer who entered therapy with me after her father died of alcoholism. When she asked me how to "break out of her anger," I pointed out that her question, not her anger, was the problem. The only answers she was interested in were suggestions for "breaking out of the anger." I did not want to confirm for her, even indirectly, that it is possible to overpower her feelings. She needed to accept her anger first. ✓

This is a subtle point, and we shall return to it many times. When Jane was willing to acknowledge her anger only because she thought this would help her get beyond it more quickly, nothing changed for her. It was only when she accepted the anger as part of who she is that she felt its full force and was able to begin putting it into true perspective. When ✓ she no longer tried to overpower her anger but instead allowed it to be exactly as deep as it was, she found that it no longer controlled her in the same way.

Jane needed to accept that there is a time for anger, a time to refrain from embracing, even a time to hate. Only after she accepted that there is a season for *all* of her feelings could she begin experiencing the time to heal as well. With healing, she will stop trying to overpower her anger. As her ✓ attitude toward anger changes, Jane will find new ways of responding to it. She will find people who won't try to "fix" her anger for her, and she will begin to express the anger directly rather than indirectly through sarcasm or passive resistance. These avenues are hidden from her as long as she relates to her anger by trying to "break out of it."

Cultivating the willingness to recover is a discipline. In practicing this discipline we discover that new attitudes begin to sprout and grow. Recovery resembles a Zen approach to life: it can never be forced; it can only be nurtured and encouraged. Recovery means getting out of the driver's seat on occasion and accepting that some aspects of our lives can proceed quite well without our having to control them with our conscious minds.

As an ACA, you may feel uncomfortable with having nothing to do to *make* recovery happen. It may be hard for you to accept that the essence of recovery lies in a change of attitude. There are things you can do to make healing more likely, just as there are things you can do to make a flower more likely to flourish. But there is nothing you can do to make it grow tall and perfect.

While the discipline of recovery can be studied, it will never work its healing power within you until it is practiced. No amount of studying, planning, and intellectual preparation will ever accomplish as much as action. There is no goal to be reached that marks a point at which you can stop practicing the discipline. If practice is abandoned, the rewards already gained can slip away with amazing speed. One aspect of recovery is to recognize and accept this reality.

Although rewards that come from recovery are great, the steps that must be taken along the way are not always easy to remain committed to. Sometimes recovery can feel like trudging across an endless desert or sinking into a bottomless pit. At these times we need to be reminded that recovery is concerned with *how* we journey through our lives, not with our final destinations.

Recovery is an attitude. It is a belief that no situation is so bad that it cannot be improved. If recovery turns into a painful chore and we feel lost, it is often because secretly we are pursuing recovery in order to gain greater control over our lives. Recovery undertaken for this motive will never bring real healing. It is only when the journey is undertaken for its own sake that rewards begin to come freely. The gift of healing stems from the attitude we take toward the journey, not from how far or how fast we can travel. If this is difficult to understand, it's because this way of looking at things is so contrary to the way in which we, as children from alcoholic homes, have been taught to think about our world—that is, it is contrary to our belief that internal peace can be gained only by getting everything in our world under control.

The journey can be undertaken in bitterness and fear, or it can be undertaken with dignity. There is a popular song, "The Greatest Love of All," that has become an unofficial anthem for the National Association for Children of Alcoholics. One line in this song reminds us that "no matter what they take from me, they can't take away my dignity." Remembering that our sense of dignity can never be touched by the behavior of others around us (including our parents) is part of recovery. The steps to recovery are designed to foster a constant awareness that dignity arises from within. It stems from maintaining your own integrity and being rigidly honest with yourself. Remaining in denial about your parent's alcoholism and about how it continues to affect your life will slowly but inevitably erode this integrity.

Recovery cannot take place in isolation. During your childhood, you lived through a time to keep silent. Your home may have been too dangerous a place to speak the truth or to talk openly about your feelings. But the road to recovery brings a time to speak. Surrounding yourself with people who remind you that you have control over your own dignity, no matter what else might be out of your control, is part of recovery. Taking the journey requires that you begin trusting others enough to depend on them for help and support. Recovery is something we must do together, whether through therapy, Twelve-Step programs, or reliance on other recover-

ing communities. Trying to recover on your own is evidence
that you are still controlled by attitudes that do not nurture
healing. As you accept the need to be part of a recovering
community, these attitudes begin to change. If this, too, is
difficult to understand, that is because it is so contrary to the
way those of us from alcoholic homes were taught to think
about ourselves and our world. We were taught that life goes
better when we hide our fears and problems from others—
especially from those whom we love and need the most.

The changes in attitude that lead to recovery occur at
such a depth that eventually they will change your self-image.
For many CoAs, a sense of inadequacy is part of their very
identities before recovery begins. You may currently think of
yourself primarily in terms of what you are not (for example,
beautiful, rich, or famous) than of what you are. Later, you
will begin to identify more fully with exactly who you are.

We all become quite attached to our images of ourselves,
even when these images are downgrading and harshly judgmental. Our self-concepts become comfortable old shoes very
quickly, and their familiarity gives them an "intuitive" feel
of correctness. But until you accept that there is a time to stop
judging yourself harshly and to start embracing yourself just
as you are, the time to heal is not yet fully at hand. It was
this sort of unconditional acceptance that we all needed from
our parents but that was prevented by the disease of alcoholism. Soon, you will be giving this acceptance to yourself.

Changes in identity (especially changes in how much we
believe is under our control) take discipline and time, and
they are inevitably experienced as upheavals. Although freedom comes with healing, it is nonetheless a time of considerable confusion, anxiety, and disorientation. It is a time to
mourn, as well as a time to dance.

You may find a variety of emotions emerging while you
read this book. You may feel sadness, anger, even fear. It's
important that you allow these feelings to emerge. They are
signs that you've come in contact with a hidden memory,
perhaps a long-forgotten trauma. It is almost impossible to

deal a final deathblow to feelings that we had as children. Our
best efforts to forget old feelings or to think them away only
serve to bury them alive. It always comes as a surprise when ✓
we roll back the stone covering their tombs and find that our
feelings from the past are still as intense as they were two,
three, four, or more decades ago. Apparently, time alone does
not heal emotional pain. And, contrary to our beliefs, all of
our conscious efforts to control and change our feelings have
had little effect on them. The reality is that our intellect has
far less control over our emotional destinies than we would
like to believe.

Perhaps you'll want to put down this book for a while
and seek out a friend for a few moments of comfort. The idea
is not to become lost in the past but to find a way of digesting
it in small doses. There is no victory in finishing the book as
quickly as possible and putting it up on the shelf like a
trophy. The goal is real healing.

You will give real healing its best chance when you read
through the following pages with enough deliberation to develop a sense of empathy for the child you were and for all
those in your family who have been affected by the disease
of alcoholism.

Today there is a new sense of hopefulness surrounding
the words "children of alcoholics." We *can* begin recovering
from the effects of being raised by an alcoholic or drug-
addicted parent.* For healing and recovery to begin, we must
be willing to look more realistically at the wounds we continue

---

*Throughout this book the word *alcoholism* can be generalized to include
all forms of chemical dependence, whether it is the abuse of alcohol,
prescription drugs, illegal drugs, or a combination of all three. Many
readers will also identify with ACA characteristics as a result of growing
up in families that were troubled by problems other than chemical dependence, such as mental illness, destructive compulsions, chronic physical
illness, or physical and sexual abuse. The lessons being learned by ACAs
regarding recovery are of general value, and should be applied wherever
useful.

to bear. We must understand where our wounds originated, as well as how we inadvertently keep them raw years longer than is necessary. We now know that Huck Finn symbolizes not only the pain and fears of being a CoA but also the strengths CoAs possess. Today, children of alcoholics can enter into a process of recovery with the assurance that real healing is possible. No one gave this promise to Huck, and no one gave this promise to you when you were a child. But today does bring you this promise.

2.

~~~~~~~~~~~~~~~~

A Time to See: Pulling Down the Walls of Denial

Before the journey of recovery can begin, you must conceive of it as a possibility and acknowledge its necessity. The primary barrier to this beginning is called *denial*.

Many children of alcoholics find that denial begins to break down only after they reach adulthood. Often, their first information about being a child of alcoholic parents comes from the general media—perhaps a newspaper article about the National Association for Children of Alcoholics, a magazine interview with a celebrity who is an ACA, or a television news segment on the growing self-help movement among ACAs. Others may find themselves intrigued by a book they happen to spot while browsing in a bookstore or by the title of a lecture they see advertised. Still others find themselves confronted with information about ACAs as a result of attending family night at a treatment center where their parent, child, spouse, or sibling has been admitted for chemical dependence. Increasingly, ACAs are being introduced to the topic by recovering friends who have developed the ability to talk openly about themselves.

Why is new information being listened to after so many years of denial? First, it has been easier to maintain the denial in the past precisely because there has been so little information available about CoAs. Second, the recently developed label, *adult children of alcoholics*, has incredible power. Many ACAs feel deeply touched by having the child within acknowledged. Part of the value of this new label is that it simultaneously acknowledges both the adult and the child in every ACA. Many ACAs, even some of those in deep denial, are aware of a strange split within themselves between how competent they may look on the outside and how much at a loss they feel internally. By seeing themselves referred to as adult children, they often gain a sudden sense that someone else understands their experience. This information—that there are other people who share similar feelings—kindles a sense of hope.

Because denial is defined in a negative way—that is, as the absence of awareness—it is difficult to look at directly. Although denial is a universal human characteristic, defining it is as difficult as explaining vision to someone who has been blind since birth or as explaining sobriety to someone who is drunk.

However, denial plays such a central role in the life of every alcoholic family, including all the children, that it is imperative to understand its effect on your life. As long as denial is allowed free rein, it will completely overwhelm your efforts to make even the first steps toward healing. Despite the difficulty of pulling down the walls of something you may not yet see, you must begin.

We are all aware of the extra sensitivity to food we feel when we're hungry. We notice every bakery and restaurant we pass, every advertisement for food we see. The hunger is like a flashlight that highlights places where food is available. This enhanced awareness, which stems from an internal preoccupation with finding food, is the opposite of what happens when denial is at work.

Denial stems from an internal preoccupation with avoiding pain. It is like a flashlight that works in reverse, casting shadows rather than light. It throws darkness over selected parts of the world to make them less noticeable, enabling us to hide embarrassing parts of our personality from our own vision, even though these parts may be obvious to everyone else. This is precisely what happens to alcoholics when they are in denial about their drinking and about the problems it causes. In short, denial prevents us from seeing things that make us too uncomfortable.

What makes denial so difficult to understand is the uncanny ability it gives us to block very specific things from of our awareness. We may put someone else's needs first and be in denial about the hurt and anger we feel at having our own needs neglected. We may allow our boss to overwork us on impossible projects and be in denial about the option we have of whether to accept the work load. We may even visit a hospitalized parent who is being treated for bleeding ulcers stemming from drinking, yet still be in denial about that parent's alcoholism.

Sometimes denial takes on power by its very audacity. Several ACAs have told me of having walked into a room as a child and seen a parent gulping a drink straight from the bottle. One embarrassed parent told his child that he had really been pouring the bottle down the drain. Suddenly, the accuracy of the child's perceptions is called into doubt. The world becomes very uncertain and confusing when you can no longer believe your own eyes.

Of course, denial is also a normal and valuable part of our lives. After we have learned of a loved one's death, we often experience a sense of unreality. Later we may hear ourselves saying, "I know she's dead, but I still don't really believe it." A part of us might even be hoping against all odds that someone will call and say it's not true. This healthy use of denial protects us from feeling the full impact of a loss all at once. Later still, we may begin to cry during a commercial for the telephone company, when images of families and friends cause the reality of our loss to intrude into our awareness. By denying potentially overwhelming feelings access to our awareness, we give ourselves the chance to break their full impact down into smaller chunks that we can digest one at a time.

Without denial, our lives would become paralyzed. It is hard to plan seriously for the future while being fully aware that there are nuclear missiles somewhere in the world programmed to explode within a few miles of where you are sitting right now. We prevent this knowledge from disrupting our lives by keeping it out of our awareness most of the time. Similarly, CoAs have to avoid being fully aware of the potential explosiveness of their parent's alcoholism in order to maintain some semblance of normality in their daily lives.

Although denial is an essential part of our lives, the potential for abusing its power is always present. This happens when denial becomes habitual and automatic. Eventually, it even casts its shadow of unawareness upon itself. When this happens, people become blind to the fact that they are blind. They deny that they are in denial. Layers upon layers of insensitivity to their feelings develop. This is why you may have reached adulthood with no awareness at all of the pervasive ways in which your parent's alcoholism has affected your life, your personality, and your very identity.

Although denial creates its own mental blind spot that prevents us from seeing its existence, the following list may help you in discerning, if only by inference, your own denial.

The Warning Signs of Denial

Level I: Your Parents' Alcoholism

- Defending your parents when other people bring their alcoholism to your attention.
- Excusing your parents' drinking ("They work hard"; "They're retired now"; "What else is there to do?").
- Hiding your parents' drinking from others.

- Speaking in euphemisms ("social drinkers," "heavy drinkers," and so on).

Level II: The Effect of Parental Alcoholism on You

- Refusing to acknowledge that your parents' alcoholism has had a major influence on your life.
- Defending your parents by taking sole responsibility for any problems stemming from your childhood.
- Not having any feelings about your parents' alcoholism.

Level III: The Excessive Use of Willpower

- Not letting yourself feel angry.
- Trying to rise above it all.
- Feeling superior to your parents.
- Taking full control of your own life, as though the alcoholism did not exist.

Unresolved feelings build up when denial is active, and they inevitably sink into your personality in ways that diminish the quality of your adult life. Of course, whether our parents are alcoholic or not, we are all pervasively affected by the families in which we grew up. Children enter their adult years with the rituals, the values, and the beliefs of their parents, or else they rebel against these rituals, values, and beliefs. Therefore, to believe that CoAs are not affected by having grown up in an alcoholic family would be to ignore the basis of all psychology and would probably be evidence of denial.

My experience, both clinically and personally, demonstrates that immense benefits come from ending the denial about being a CoA. The legacy of an alcoholic family can be a heavy burden during adulthood until the silence about the past is discarded and buried feelings are exposed to the light of awareness. Early years spent in chaos, denial, and fear provide tools that are useful for survival. But when survival skills become automatic reflexes, they begin to be used in every part of your life, even when they are inappropriate and no longer needed.

Helen, a former client, is an example of how denial can prevent a CoA from entering into recovery. In her own words, "I identified my sister as a child of an alcoholic three months before I realized that I'm an ACA, too!" In the therapy with her, it became clear that her denial had two major roots: her family saw denial as normal behavior, and Helen had a profound sense of shame and bitterness that flooded her emotions whenever she got close to acknowledging the truth. To understand the role that denial played in her life and to pull down its walls, Helen had to begin—as all ACAs must—by learning more about alcoholism itself.

THE DISEASE OF ALCOHOLISM

Alcoholism, like other chemical dependencies, is a disease. Most people, including many alcoholics and ACAs, have difficulty accepting this fact. Almost everyone believes that the central problem for alcoholics is a lack of willpower. Common sense may tell us this, but common sense is wrong. We need to remember that common sense also told people that the earth was flat and that the sun revolved around the earth. Today, it mistakenly tells many people that AIDS is punishment for homosexuality and that alcoholics are getting what they deserve for being so weak.

Alcoholism can be genetically inherited. At least 50 percent of all alcoholics have an alcoholic parent. As many as 25 percent of CoAs become addicted to alcohol and other drugs, *whether they grow up with their alcoholic parents or are adopted at birth into nonalcoholic families.*

Once a person is addicted to alcohol, his or her brain chemistry enters a state that no amount of willpower can alter. Alcohol creates mood swings, impairs coordination, decreases memory, and even diminishes problem-solving abilities. *All of these effects last long after a person is no longer actively drunk.*

A master auto mechanic once explained that he entered recovery from his alcoholism when he recognized that his ability to troubleshoot engine problems was deteriorating. He described the growing tendency that he'd had to get one idea in his mind (for example, "the carburetor is the problem") and to not be able to shift to other possibilities if his first idea proved wrong. He would go back and recheck the carburetor, while his students went on to the next most likely source of the problem. Unfortunately, it is precisely this ability to look at things in a different light that is necessary for alcoholics to be able to recognize their denial about the ways in which drinking diminishes the quality of their lives.

Alcoholism is a disease involving a great deal of denial, and most alcoholics present a facade to the world—a representation of themselves as not being alcoholic. They are quick to point to all the evidence that proves they are not alcoholic. One person argues that she can't be an alcoholic because she never drinks alone, as alcoholics do. Another says that he can't be one because he only drinks beer. Yet another says that she has never missed a day of work because of drinking, so she certainly isn't an alcoholic.

This rationalization can assume preposterous proportions. One recovering alcoholic said that he used to sit at his kitchen table with bottle and glass ready, waiting for the clock to reach noon. In his mind, only alcoholics drank in the morning. Such a facade of normality results from years of denying reality, both to oneself and to others.

The symptoms of alcoholism are so numerous that no single person can have them all. Naturally, then, alcoholics can point to things that "typical" alcoholics do that are not true of them. This is especially true when their definition of an alcoholic is someone who drinks more than they do.

ACAs also get caught up in denying their parents' alcoholism. Over and over, I have heard ACAs talk of having put their parents to bed or of having pulled them out of bars before they could be arrested, only to have the ACAs then lapse into doubting that their parents were really alcoholics. As ACAs, we learned early on to ignore the evidence and to concentrate instead on the reasons why our parents were not really alcoholics. After all, we may say, our parents never ended up on skid row. Denial.

Whenever the use of alcohol becomes a habitual part of people's lives, there is a risk that it is substituting for internal growth in their personalities. The facade they use to confront the world prevents them from becoming psychologically complete. As they become more distant from themselves, the possibility for intimacy with others, including their children, erodes.

Any attempt on your part to point to alcohol as the real cause of a worsening relationship with an alcoholic is seen as an attack. The alcoholic becomes defensive and tries to get you to feel guilty for accusing him or her of something horrible. The topic of drinking is closed to discussion, and if you try to open the discussion again you are portrayed as a troublemaker. Often, you begin to doubt whether you were right.

Denial is contagious. Out of a sense of shame, many families cooperate with keeping the alcoholic's facade intact. A conspiracy of silence about the real problem spreads through the entire family and keeps each member from speaking the truth to the outside world, to each other, or even to themselves. They make excuses to neighbors, relatives, bosses, and the police for the alcoholic's behavior. Children learn to make excuses to their teachers for their parents' absence at PTA meetings, just as they have seen excuses given to employers.

In many families, the children are focused on as a facade. The children's good behavior and good grades at school become part of the family's pretense that nothing is wrong. How could there be anything wrong in a family with such fine kids? In other families, the children's misconduct and bad grades are pointed to as the "real" problem in the family.

One ACA, Robert, told me with some justifiable pride that he already knew at age eleven what his job was whenever the family moved. He would immediately locate the nearest hardware store, buy paint and brushes, and paint the front of the house. He painted only the front because he knew that the family would be moving again in another six months. Even at age eleven, Robert understood how to help his family put up a good front.

It should come as no surprise that today, as an adult, Robert has trouble dropping the pretense that his life is completely in order. This facade is a false self. It prevents Robert from talking honestly about the sense of worthlessness that silently plagues him. He is too ashamed to talk about anything he thinks is a sign of weakness. But, as with all ACAs, until he is able to talk about these things openly they will remain part of the fabric of his life.

THE THREE LEVELS OF DENIAL

There are three levels of denial that children of alcoholics must ultimately confront in themselves. Level I is denial of the basic fact that a parent is an alcoholic. A host of alternative terms is used: problem drinker, social drinker, heavy drinker, and so on. Each of these is an attempt to minimize the reality and to avoid having feelings about a parent's being an alcoholic. Since children of alcoholics tend to share their family's judgmental view of alcoholism, denial that a parent is alcoholic keeps you from having to make negative judgments about someone you love.

Level II of denial is seen in people who do acknowledge that a parent is alcoholic but who insist that the alcoholism has had little effect on the rest of the family. There is complete denial that the rest of the family has anything to recover from. There is denial that anyone other than the alcoholic participated in the self-destruction of living behind a facade, in isolation and silence. The nonalcoholic parent, if there is one, may be seen as faultless. If your alcoholic parent has died or left the family, you may attempt to divorce yourself from ever needing that parent. Such a tactic protects you from feeling pain, but it truly does violence to one of your most basic human emotions—the yearning for parental love and acceptance. More harm is ultimately done by disowning this yearning than by having it frustrated.

Level III of denial exists if you acknowledge both that your parent is alcoholic and that the alcoholism also affected the rest of the family, but you still feel that through force of will you can control the damage in your own life by burying it as deeply as possible. One of the questions most commonly asked by ACAs is, "Why should I open all of this up again? It's not bothering me now, and talking about it just feels like opening up an old wound." This reveals an underlying belief that it is possible to keep the past from affecting your life merely by refusing to let it.

But feelings that have been buried alive continue to be alive. They do not necessarily fade with the passage of time. We simply get better at ignoring the feelings by forgetting much of the past—including such things as physical or sexual abuse. We deny our feelings, just as our parents denied that alcohol was affecting their lives.

To understand how fully alive these feelings remain, simply pay attention to the passions that are unleashed when you begin to face your childhood honestly: anger, sadness, shame, bitterness, abandonment, and feeling out of control. These are the repressed passions of childhood. They have waited a long time to emerge.

The sheer strength of these leftover feelings is often used as an excuse for maintaining your denial. But if you choose to ignore them further, you will be treating them with the same disregard that came from the rest of your family when you were a child. Someone needs to listen to them, and validate them, someday. It might as well start with you.

All of these levels of denial have the same consequence. Once you deny the real source of your feelings, your pain becomes sourceless, and no amount of searching for freedom from the pain has a chance to succeed until your feelings are acknowledged. This sourceless sense of discomfort is frequently seen in active alcoholics as well. Since denial prevents them from seeing alcohol as the source of their problems, any negative consequences from their drinking must be ascribed to something else. This process of trying to discover a plausible cause for pain, when the real cause is hidden behind a wall of denial, is called rationalization. Children of alcoholics still in denial try to make sense of their feelings, but they simply lack the essential piece needed to complete the puzzle. You can end up dealing more with rationalizations for your pain than you do with its real cause. As a result, you get caught on the level of your facade—your false self—and lose access to the level of your true self.

The only explanation for why we remain in denial, even when it continues to cause us pain, is the powerful fear we all have of the unknown. As ACAs, we grew up with the threat of unknown catastrophes lurking in the shadows nearby. A parent could go on a binge at any moment. Tonight could be the night that mother never comes home. Uncertainty permeated everything that happened in your home. As an ACA, you face the uncertainty that comes from opening up feelings that have been denied awareness since your childhood. You may have a number of questions at this point: "What feelings will I have to face? How deep do they run? Will they overwhelm me?"

We learned how to tolerate feeling uncomfortable

around our parents' drinking in order to avoid rocking the boat and risking making things even worse. We were even rewarded for helping to keep the family's secret, since everyone feared that it would only make things worse if others knew about our parents' alcoholism. Our childhoods were lived in an atmosphere in which it was a betrayal to speak the truth. Denial became everyone's way of containing fear of the unknown.

When so much of your early life is spent hiding emotions, you enter adult life afraid to let your true feelings be seen even by yourself. There is often a conviction that deep feelings can only be allowed to surface when you are alone. The beginning of recovery from the worst effects of being a CoA comes when this conviction is given up. The truth is that some feelings are easier to have in the presence of other people than when you are alone. ACAs are frequently confused about when it is all right to need other people and when it is not. There are no clear lines, no points of reference, for knowing how to be in a relationship without losing your sense of self.

The process of recovery involves recognizing that many feelings you had as a child were never listened to and respected by your parents. Perhaps these feelings were too painful for them to see. Perhaps they were too focused on their own problems. Perhaps they were too drunk or were physically absent. The final effect was that your feelings were buried alive, but their intensity has remained unabated. Over the years, more and more energy has had to be used to keep things submerged. Despite efforts to keep your old feelings under control, they have inevitably spilled over into other parts of your life, creating problems that seem to have no connection to your parent's alcoholism.

A Time to Heal is based on the belief that every ACA can benefit from becoming more aware of the realities of the past, including the realities of how it felt to be locked into that past as a child. Every ACA can benefit from making the past

real, from finally ending the denial that started to protect a
parent's drinking or to sanitize memories of early family life.
For some ACAs, this journey inward may prove to be lifesav-
ing. For others, it may simply supply a missing piece in the
puzzle of their lives. In all cases, there is no reality so bad
that we are better off denying it. We lose more by abandoning
our awareness of the facts than we can ever lose by facing
whatever those facts might be.

Part 2

The Road Behind

The first two chapters have brought us to a point at which a leap of faith is required before we can go any further. The promise of healing has been offered, if you are willing to enter into the discipline of recovery. The first step in this discipline is a willingness to relinquish denial. This step will permit you to take a more realistic look at your past and how it continues to mold your present.

There is a world of difference between reading or thinking about relinquishing your denial and actually doing it. This is where the leap of faith is demanded. Your denial helped protect you during your childhood, and it has probably remained active during much of your adult life as well. To relinquish it now will leave you more vulnerable than you have allowed yourself to be for a long time. You will be vulnerable to your memories. You will be vulnerable to all of your feelings. And you will be vulnerable to the truth.

Although I can promise that there will be much relief and real healing as you make progress in recovery, I have no proof to offer ahead of time that this promise will be fulfilled. The closest you can come to a guarantee is to talk to other ACAs who have already spent time in recovery. The next section presents my best understanding of the childhood experience of ACAs, as seen with a minimum of denial obscuring our perspective. If any of what you read in the next pages rings true with your own memories, perhaps the leap of faith facing you will become a bit easier.

It would be denial to pretend that such a leap is not scary. Those who wait for their fear to fade before beginning to dismantle their denial can wait a lifetime. If you accept that the leap must be made in the face of your fear, then there is little reason to put it off much longer. The following chapters outline much of what I think you might see if you are willing to let the past be real.

3.

A Time to Remember: Childhood in an Alcoholic Family

At conferences, I often illustrate the emotional charge ACAs feel about their families by saying one word: "Dinnertime." And my point is made. The reaction is invariably a mixture of laughter and groans from ACAs in the audience. Few moments are as stressful for children of alcoholics as when their families try to come together at the end of a day to share a meal.

Deborah tells of the terror she felt as a youngster when dinnertime approached. The evening meal became the focal point of her day. If she was going to have any contact with her father, a college professor, it would be then. Her father dominated the table by directing a barrage of questions at his children regarding their schoolwork. Only on rare occasions was Deborah able to answer to his satisfaction. These moments of his approval gave her an inner glow that lasted until the next dinnertime, when she had to prove herself all over again. On most days, her father was able to reveal her "ignorance" within the first few questions, causing Deborah to feel bitterly disappointed with herself. She remembers feeling that she was so inadequate that she was not even worthy of being tested in these daily interrogations.

The worst nights were when her father, completely withdrawn, would sit sullenly and say almost nothing during the entire meal. Her mother would nervously take over and attempt to fill the silence with a steady stream of small talk about school activities and social functions. To Deborah, her mother seemed vacuous and continually anxious.

These dinnertime memories came up again and again throughout the course of Deborah's recovery. She began to remember more clearly the knot of tension in her stomach that followed disappointing her father once again, and she remembered how she felt when her father forced her to finish everything on her plate without complaining. These memories began to help her make sense of her chronic intestinal problems and of her frequent binging on sweets and desserts. As Deborah continued to explore what it had felt like to be sitting at her father's table as a terrified eight-year-old, her perfectionism and her overemphasis on achieving intellectual competence at the cost of emotional growth began to lessen for the first time in her life.

Most importantly, when Deborah stopped denying how much her father's behavior at mealtime was affected by alcohol, she was able to make new sense of her life. As a child, she had been totally puzzled by her father's moods. She constantly thought she was the cause of his irritability or that she had chased her father away into his silence. It was only in therapy as an adult that Deborah was able to see the connection between his moods and his drinking. When her father was controlling his drinking to avoid his wife's criticism, the tension between himself and his wife mounted until he became oblivious to the needs of the family and retreated into sullen silence. As an adult, Deborah was able to see that his brooding moods had actually been signs of the early stages of his alcoholism and that they had had nothing to do with her personally.

Alex related a much more traumatic dinner scene. His alcoholic mother was married at the time to a man who became very abusive, verbally and physically, when he was intoxicated. Otherwise, he was charming, and he loved to play with Alex for hours. Unfortunately, Alex's stepfather usually began drinking at dinnertime, which led to vicious arguments by the end of the meal on an almost daily basis. Alex learned to eat quickly and to find excuses to leave the table as soon as possible.

On his mother's birthday, Alex made a special effort to help ensure that the day would go well. Although he was only in the second grade, he went alone to the grocery store to buy food for the dinner. He knew that his mother would probably start drinking early in the day to celebrate her birthday, so he took full responsibility for putting a special dinner on the table. When his mother passed out and fell face first into her plate before the birthday cake had been served, his stepfather began to berate her for not being able to stay sober long enough to enjoy the dinner Alex had prepared. He pushed her off her chair in order to wake her, and a physical brawl followed.

Alex ran from the house in tears. He was convinced he was to blame for the fight. The first cross words his mother had spoken were toward him, demanding that he give her a napkin. Alex had set the table and served the entire meal himself, but he had forgotten to put napkins on the table. For the next three decades he berated himself for having done an inadequate job. His seven-year-old mind accepted the entire blame for the terrible fight that night.

UNDERLEARNING

The legacy from growing up in an alcoholic home comes as much from what did not happen as from what did. As an ACA, you can reach adulthood without being exposed to even the most elementary things. You may never have had friends stay overnight at your house or visit during the day. You may never have seen guests at your family's dinner table. You may never have seen your family gathered at the dinner table. You may never have seen a Thanksgiving celebration, had a birthday party, or been on a family vacation. Even basic social skills—such as meal preparation, housekeeping, and personal hygiene—may have been seriously neglected. Effective work attitudes may be completely foreign concepts. Financial responsibility might never have been witnessed. You may never have seen an argument that was resolved and that did not lead to physical violence. You may never have seen an intimate relationship between two separate individuals . . . and on and on. The list is unique for each ACA.

ACAs are left to reinvent the wheel in countless ways, without the aid of a blueprint or a picture, as they make their way through this world. Doug, a successful financial consultant, told of having been embarrassed while buying a pair of shoes to go with his new suit. The salesclerk looked up, after trying to untie Doug's shoes, and asked, "Where did you learn to tie your shoes?" Doug was forty-three years old, and he was being told by a clerk half his age that he did not know how to tie his shoes right. A wave of shame swept over him as the clerk taught him the usual way men tie their shoelaces. It was only later that Doug remembered the scene when his alcoholic mother had grown impatient while teaching him to tie his shoes when he was five. She had cuffed him on the side of the head and told him to figure it out himself. Doug went outdoors and worked at it until he figured out a way to tie his laces tight enough to keep his shoes on. He was a victim of underlearning.

— By *underlearning* I am referring to the random, unexpected gaps in experience that affect ACAs. Because underlearning, like denial, creates its own blind spots (if you don't know what's normal, how do you know that you are not?), you can use the following twelve signs to help you determine whether you are a victim of underlearning.

Twelve Signs of Underlearning

1. Constantly guessing at what "normal" is.
2. Wondering what you "ought" to be feeling in different situations.

3. Excessive fear of the unknown.
4. Overreliance on watching other people to see how you should be acting.
5. Feeling at a loss when you get married or when your first child is born.
6. Running to self-improvement books whenever change happens in your life.
7. Believing that others usually know what they're doing.
8. Always deferring to others to plan vacations, dinners, parties, and so on.
9. Feeling like you are pulling the wool over people's eyes.
10. Making "big deals" about things other people do easily.
11. Neglecting such things as daily chores and financial records out of ignorance.
12. Frequently being surprised by learning that there are simple ways to accomplish things that you do in convoluted ways.

ACAs often do not know what normal adults are supposed to be like because their vision of mature behavior, which most people get from watching their parents, is incomplete. Their families have not provided them with all the models of healthy, or even civil, adult behavior that are needed.

When you feel like a foreigner in a strange land, with no knowledge of its customs and common courtesies, you continually look to other people to know what is appropriate to feel or do in a particular situation. You learn to pass for normal, all the while assuming that everyone else knows exactly what normal is. All too often, an ACA's only idea of normalcy is that it means not having any problems.

Children of alcoholics are often either unaware that their vision of mature behavior is truncated or are too embarrassed to let others see that they are unsure about what is normal.

When your vision of mental health is stunted, the sense of dissatisfaction in your life has no clear source. Instead of trying to determine how you might live your life differently (which would require having a clear picture of more authentic behavior), you criticize yourself for not being able to be content with your life. You attempt to compromise and settle for mere survival. When your spirit cannot be contained and you feel the ache of being only half alive, you redouble your self-criticism. You deny the pain of being stunted in your relationships with yourself and with others, hoping that the status quo will stay tolerable.

The other way to compensate for not being "normal" is to become an astute observer and imitator of other people. This leads to your having a very competent facade, such that even your closest friends probably have no inkling of the fact that you are simply acting "as if." But as long as you are choosing actions and feelings to reflect what you imagine to be normal, your experience can never go beyond feeling *as if* you are normal. As close as you might get in appearance, the feeling of being a real part of the world will never be yours in any deep way.

The idea that normalcy is a set of rules that can be discovered and adopted like a new set of clothes is a deeply flawed notion. It leads ACAs on an endless wild-goose chase, searching through one self-help book after another, one growth-enhancing course after another, to one savior after another in their search for answers. Many ACAs salve the pain of having searched in vain for rules to follow by taking on the identity of the lonely pilgrim who never reaches his goal but who is always packing up his belongings one more time to continue the noble journey.

Many children, like Alex, have tremendous gaps in their experiences. Alex's family life lacked any continuity and was unsafe; there was no respect for his feelings, and there was never any direct communication about anything. Alex learned that the world was capricious and dangerous, and he learned how to survive in that world. What he did not learn was that a whole different world existed outside his family. The only glimpses he had of this came from the unreality of television situation comedies. "Father Knows Best" and "Leave It to Beaver" were the closest Alex had come to experiencing a healthy family life, and he naturally assumed that these were only fictional.

As an adult, Alex knew that his ways of relating to his feelings and to other people were not working. However, before he could develop a more satisfying relationship with his girlfriend, he needed to learn what the elements of an intimate relationship were. Until then, he was navigating through life without the usual maps to guide him.

In the most severe instances, underlearning can narrow the horizons for ACAs until their lives need more repair than they can accomplish alone. Without significant help from the outside, many of them will never find the peace of mind they so desperately seek. Fortunately, such help is now available, and you do not have to wait passively for this help to arrive. Part 3 will explore the types of help you can find for yourself. But before we get to that point, you must prepare yourself to receive the full benefit of this help.

CHARACTERISTICS OF HEALTHY FAMILIES

Perhaps the best way to understand the numerous ways in which alcoholism pervasively affects family life and betrays the trust children naturally place in their parents is to look at the characteristics of healthy families. If you are an ACA, it is possible that you have never had experience with a family that is operating effectively. The table on page 57 summarizes many of the characteristics of a healthy family, followed by how these characteristics are disrupted in alcoholic families.

No family contains all of these characteristics all of the

time. However, most healthy families demonstrate these characteristics more often than not, particularly during times of
stress. In fact, what makes these families function well is that
they are less likely than alcoholic families to be overwhelmed
by stress, since they cope more effectively with the problems
stress causes. Invariably, the impact of parental alcoholism is
to diminish the ability of a family to sustain the following
healthy characteristics.

Safety

Children are born into this world unable to take care of their
basic needs. (Healthy families provide whatever is needed to
protect the physical and emotional safety of children. At first,
this means assuring warm and dry shelter, healthy food, and
proper hygiene. Later, it means ensuring physical restraints
and proper limits to minimize accidents and to assure that
children encounter only those challenges that are within their
capabilities. Safety for a child also includes having the relative certainty that the people who surround him are emotionally available, particularly at times when the child is overwhelmed. It means that a child never needs to worry about
whether or not her parents can restrain their own aggressive
and hostile impulses. None of these safety factors may hold
true for the child of an alcoholic.

Alcoholism in a parent gradually erodes, and can eventually destroy, a child's sense of safety. It is almost universally
true that people become increasingly self-centered when
drinking. The anesthetic qualities of the drug make all of us
less aware of subtle stimuli, including the usual cues from
other people that they want our attention. Children feel less
safe when they sense that their parents are unable to focus
on anyone else's needs. In some cases, parents may assume
that the child's feelings are the same as theirs. In other cases,
they may either ignore or ridicule the child's feelings or
withdraw completely from any emotional attachment to the

Characteristics of Healthy Families	Disruptions Caused by Parental Alcoholism
Safety	Emotional unavailability of parent Loss of control in a parent Failure to protect children from hazards Direct physical abuse
Open Communication	Secrets kept to keep the peace Facade of normality maintained Feelings hidden Children made into confidants
Self-Care	"Scarcity" economy Alcoholic's needs come first Feeling responsible for other people's problems
Individualized Roles	Family's needs dictate roles Roles become rigid, especially during times of stress
Continuity	Chaos Arbitrariness Dissolution of the family
Respect for Privacy	Parents become intrusive Secrets confused with privacy No respect for individual differences
Focused Attention Schedule	Determined by the alcoholism, not the child's needs
Quality	Restricted range of emotions available Alcohol-affected emotions never reach resolution

child. This withdrawal can last anywhere from a few minutes to an entire lifetime. When parents can no longer be reached emotionally, children feel a deep sense of abandonment.

Children are very sensitive to the loosening of self-restraint that occurs when their parents become intoxicated. There is probably nothing more terrifying to a child than to be around a parent who is truly out of control. Since alcoholism means, by definition, that a person has lost control over his or her drinking, CoAs live in constant danger of having their worlds fly apart. While this may sound overly dramatic, it is not. After all, most alcoholics live with a similar fear, so it is not surprising that their children share this concern. And given the frequency with which alcoholism contributes to divorce, illness, and premature death, an expectation that catastrophe lies right around the corner makes sense.

Intoxicated parents often fail to protect children from everyday hazards. They do not monitor a young child's play closely enough, as in the case of an alcoholic father who allowed his five-year-old to use the family's swimming pool unattended while he drank in front of the television set. Many ACAs recall having been left alone well into the night without a baby-sitter. One ACA, Carol, remembers fixing sugar sandwiches for her younger sisters, putting them to bed, and telling them stories to quiet their fears. Carol was four years old at the time, and her mother sometimes stayed away from home for as long as three days.

As a parent's alcoholism becomes more blatant, neglect of a child's safety can be a direct threat to the child's health. Childhood immunizations may be neglected, or a parent may fail to observe a child's illness in time to get adequate medical care. I have personally seen a thirteen-year-old girl develop such severe pneumonia that she required a respirator to sustain her life, all because her parents neglected to get her to a doctor during one of their binges.

In the worst cases, parents become openly abusive of their children, either physically or sexually, or both. Child abuse occurs much more often in families where one or both of the parents are alcoholic. It is difficult to imagine any betrayal that is more poignant than that of a small child being beaten or sexually exploited by the very people he or she must depend on for emotional and physical safety. The stories of Huck Finn's abuse at the hands of his father are all too familiar to many ACAs today. When alcohol turns your parent into a bully, there are few safe places to hide, and the entire universe begins to look dangerous.

— One place that children who are physically or sexually abused do find to hide is within their own minds. Most children instinctively protect themselves from the full depth of a parent's betrayal by assuming that they somehow deserve the abuse. Although this may be hard to understand, it makes perfect sense emotionally. Assuming responsibility for your parent's abusive behavior toward you is useful in two ways. First, it gives you reason to hope that you might eventually be able to control your fate better: if you can only discover the right way to act, the abuse will stop. Children need to feel hopeful, and they are thus likely to take the blame for things that are out of their control in order to rescue a sense of hopefulness.

Second, the lack of safety in physically and sexually abusive homes affects the very identity of children, leading them to feel deeply inadequate and defective. By seeing yourself as deserving to be beaten, you can still believe your parent is good and loving. This is much harder to believe if you understand that your parent is losing control of his or her anger and randomly beating you for no particular reason. Experience with abused children tells us that it is often more important for a child to believe that their parents are faultless than to believe in their own innocence.

Open Communication

Members of functional families talk to one another freely. The underlying assumption is that the family will work best if everyone puts all of his cards on the table and if new points of view are tolerated. When people are rewarded for being assertive, problems are brought into the light of day before they have had time to fester into deep resentments; in addition, a wider range of alternative solutions are considered.

Honesty is engendered in an environment of open communication. Tempering this honesty is the parents' understanding that children need to be respected for the level of comprehension appropriate for their particular ages. Children are then communicated with openly in terms they can understand. Respect for the safety needs of children prevents parents from expecting their children to be able to deal with emotionally charged material on the same level as adults do. The need for open communication is not abused in a way that turns children into confidants for the parents' own fears.

An alcoholic family gradually comes to operate according to a different underlying assumption: that putting all the cards on the table is dangerous. Secrets are kept in the belief that if the truth were allowed out, it could lead to greater conflict or cause people to leave. The family becomes closed to any new information about itself.

Alcoholics begin the process of keeping secrets by minimizing the amount they drink. The next phase is that of actively hiding the drinking; finally, they hide from the negative consequences caused by their drinking. The other parent often tries to shield the children from the truth about the drinking, frequently out of a sense of shame. The motivation to safeguard the children cannot be faulted, but the belief that safety can be purchased by ignorance continues the slide away from open communication.

Gradually, the tendency to keep secrets seeps into other areas, until everyone in the family is hiding feelings he or she is convinced would needlessly rock the boat if they were openly aired. This atmosphere, in which family members must identify more and more with their false fronts, eventually diminishes everyone's self-esteem. Family dynamics become centered more around protecting the sanctity of secrets than protecting the integrity of the family members.

ACAs from such family environments often feel that they are breaking a rule when they speak honestly about their feelings. You may be familiar with all of the arguments you have to go through inside yourself before you can bring up a topic of conversation you think someone else might not like. It is often easier not to talk than to experience the fear that stems from open communication.

Paradoxically, alcoholic parents can also lose a sense of the distinctions that exist between themselves and their children. When intoxicated, parents often take children into their confidence in ways that both terrify children and give them a sense of a special relationship with the parent. A drunk adult may pour out his life's problems to his or her child as easily as he would to a bartender; the child is simply used as a shoulder to cry on. Little attention is paid to how the child feels about hearing all of this.

ACAs report having had to listen to alcoholic parents talk about their wish to commit suicide or about their sexual problems, in great detail. This is not open communication but rather a symptom of the total lack of boundaries between parent and child. The parent has abandoned his or her proper role in the family. When youngsters are turned into confidants, the important distinction between parent and child is blurred. One of the most bitter complaints I hear from ACAs is that their parents were never really parents for them.

Jack

Jack is a thirty-two-year-old ACA who came to me for group therapy. He was so compliant and eager to please that no one was getting to know anything about him. Whenever the focus was on him, Jack managed to turn it around and ask interesting questions about someone else in the group. If anyone disagreed with something he said or pressed him to reveal more about himself, it suddenly seemed as though no one was home anymore. Jack became emotionally vacant.

This behavior made sense once Jack described his family. Throughout Jack's childhood, his father had had the habit of staying out until the middle of the night, drinking heavily. Jack had felt terrified each evening, but he had to sit with his mother and comfort her. He listened as she alternated between expressing anger at his father and pouring out her own fears. Later, sometime in the middle of the night, Jack's father would wake him to come out into the kitchen and sit with him as he fixed a huge breakfast and told Jack all about how difficult it was for him to have to put up with Jack's mother.

Jack learned at an early age that it was his job in life to pay attention to others, whether he was interested or not, and that it was dangerous to let them know too much about what he was really thinking. His mother always felt deeply hurt if Jack was not interested in listening to her. His father simply exploded and slammed him against the wall if he did not pay attention.

Jack's story also illustrates two important points. First, as discussed earlier, open communication does not mean total honesty, regardless of a child's age. Second, Jack's story demonstrates how the nondrinking parent can also fall into inappropriately using a child as a confidant. The fact that one parent is actively alcoholic and unavailable does not make it acceptable for the other parent to slip into using the children to fill the role vacated by the spouse. In its extreme, this behavior leads to the emotional equivalent of incest, as a child intermittently becomes a surrogate spouse.

Self-Care

Families function more successfully when positive value is placed on individual members actively taking good care of themselves. At times, this will mean that one member puts increased demands on the rest of the family's time and energy, as when a parent uproots the family in order to accept a better job or when a child requires financial and emotional support from parents to pursue interests such as music or sports. At other times, it will mean that a member of the family may be less available to the others. When this stems from the member's need to "recharge" by seeking rest, solitude, the company of others outside the family, or spiritual pursuits, it is not seen as a threat by others in the family. The assumption is that every individual has the responsibility to determine what he or she needs to remain healthy and to continue growing. Such families are based on a fundamental trust that an endless supply of health and happiness exists. Whenever one family member achieves a goal, there is no fear among the others that this makes the achievement of their own goals less likely.

The scarcity economy existing in alcoholic families prevents members from taking good care of themselves. (The central belief of the scarcity economy is that there is a limited supply of anything worthwhile.) Happiness is viewed as a pizza pie: if I take a slice, that means there is less left for you. For example, alcoholic parents can become convinced that their misery comes from not receiving enough love and attention from other family members who are taking good care of themselves. This is a frequent rationalization for drinking and can easily become self-reinforcing. A person drinks to blunt the pain of not being "loved" by the spouse, who finds it more difficult to be loving when the drinking is present. Furthermore, when the nondrinking parent decides to invest more energy into maintaining his or her own health (by going to Al-Anon, for instance), this is interpreted by the drinking parent as a sign of callousness. The scarcity economy implies that there is only so much energy available for being healthy, and if you are using some of it up for your own purposes, there is less left over for me. Alcoholic families can eventually end up attacking the efforts of family members to separate from the craziness long enough to regain their own health— an act that these families perceive as abandonment.

It has often been said of alcoholic families that no one is permitted to get any healthier than the sickest member. This rule certainly controlled the first two-and-a-half decades of Albert's life. An only child, he was raised by an alcoholic father and a paranoid schizophrenic mother. His mother stayed indoors for weeks at a stretch and sometimes went for days without speaking a word. His father was never able to keep a job, so the family was forced to move three or four times a year. Albert remembers with special horror the times when the family was evicted and he had to stand guard on the sidewalk over their possessions while his parents searched for a place to live. By the time Albert was eight years old, he was expert at foraging through trash cans behind restaurants to get dinner for the family. By the age of twelve, he was bringing in as much money as his father. By fourteen, he was the sole support of the family.

For the next eleven years, Albert's parents permitted him to keep a roof over their heads and food on the table. Once Albert accepted full responsibility for supporting the family, his life settled down considerably. He no longer went hungry, and they moved far less often. Over the years, he watched his high school friends move away from their homes and begin their adult lives. Whenever Albert attempted to break away from his parents, his father went on a binge and disappeared, and his mother began screaming at strangers. Not only had Albert become the glue that kept the family unit together, but he was also needed to keep each parent "together."

It took him until his mid-twenties to make the decision to burst out of his family, no matter what the consequences might be to his parents. It had become clear that if he waited for them to be ready for him to leave, he would have to care for them for the rest of their lives. When his parents finally realized that Albert had moved 500 miles away, they wrote him off completely and acted as though he had died.

Is it any surprise that Albert has had no intimate relationships during his adult life? His need to be self-sufficient is an obsession. He has almost no basis for believing that others might be interested in his feelings or supportive of his taking good care of himself. For Albert, recovery required a leap of faith, which he took when he began talking openly in self-help meetings about his pervasive sense of loneliness and isolation.

Individualized Roles

In healthy families, the role each child fills is individualized to meet the child's unique strengths and needs. Parents can help their children in this process by maintaining clarity about their own roles as parents. Although children often fight against the boundaries set for them by their parents, this resistance is an important part of their growing up. For parents to set these boundaries effectively, they must permit children to struggle against the restraints, and they must be flexible enough to change the restraints as a child becomes capable of assuming greater responsibility.

Whenever it becomes unclear who is responsible for setting boundaries, the roles defining parents and children start to blur. This is profoundly upsetting to children. Eventually, children do outgrow their need for external containment; when parents abandon their proper roles, however, children are thrust prematurely into the world. Although they may initially enjoy the sense of license this brings, and although they may rise to the occasion and quickly adopt adult responsibility, children are nonetheless paying a price. This price is having to postpone childhood or abandon it altogether.

Anyone who reads ACA literature soon encounters two descriptions of the roles typically seen in alcoholic families. Sharon Wegscheider-Cruse identifies children as tending to fall into one of the following roles: hero, scapegoat, lost child, and mascot. Claudia Black is clearly looking at the same thing when she speaks of children who take on the roles of the responsible one, the adjuster, the placater, and the acting-out child. These descriptions have been extremely valuable for ACAs in two ways: they serve as powerful windows for seeing the underlying realities of living in an alcoholic home, and they help ACAs to accurately connect their childhood experiences with what they are like as adults.

These roles are almost universally found to some degree in all families. However, when alcohol or other illness disrupts these roles in a family, they become very rigid and emerge from the family's needs, rather than the child's.

The ties that bind people together into a family become greatly altered by the existence of an alcoholic parent. More and more, the needs of individual family members become secondary to the desperate needs of the family. Gradually, the need to have a child play a particular role becomes the family's need, whether it fits the personality of the child or not. Pressure mounts for people to fulfill roles that are dictated by circumstances rather than by their own inner growth. Furthermore, once an individual becomes identified with a particular role, less and less deviation from that role is tolerated. Whereas a healthy family might allow a child a wide range of reactions to an event, an alcoholic family denies such flexibility. In alcoholic families, people are expected to take on specific roles, especially during times of stress. The habit of playing the part that has been assigned rather than reacting more honestly erodes integrity rather than supports it.

For example, families can have very different responses

to the parents' decision to move to another town. In a healthy family, enough flexibility exists for each child to express both positive and negative feelings about the move. The parents support their children, guided by the particular needs that arise from each.

In an alcoholic family, there is an underlying sense that the family is already strained beyond its tolerance. With the decision to move, the child who has generally reacted positively to family crises is expected to take this news smoothly. In times of stress, there is no flexibility to have contrary feelings. Each family member tries to help the family by playing a familiar role. The hero is upbeat. The lost child has no feelings. The mascot makes light of the problems. The rigidity of these roles discourages everyone from being aware of whatever feelings he or she is actually having.

When children grow up rigidly identified with a single role, they become stuck in those roles as adults. Albert found it almost impossible to get out of the habit of adjusting to others, placating others, and assuming responsibility for everything that has to be done. Whenever his boss gets behind schedule as a result of poor planning, Albert immediately begins taking on more overtime work. He does not feel that he does this by choice; he feels he has to. Although he has separated physically from his parents, he has not broken the habits he developed while living with them. This is true of most ACAs.

Continuity

Healthy families serve as a source of continuity in the lives of their members, usually through an endless series of formal and informal rituals. Birthdays, weddings, funerals, holidays, weekends, vacations, and such simple things as meals and phone calls serve as touchstones you can return to over and over without fail, either in real life or in your memory. The family is something of greater scope and significance than any single individual member. When we belong to a family, we belong to something larger and older than ourselves, something with a future beyond our own life span.

Actively alcoholic parents lack continuity within their own personalities and export this discontinuity into the family as a whole. CoAs see their parents undergo sudden changes in mood and behavior that can never be predicted. A parent's anxiety about whether a job promotion will come or not can suddenly vanish, dissolved in a couple of ounces of alcohol. When feelings are dissolved artificially, they are prone to reemerge at unpredictable and arbitrary times. The result is that what a child is praised for today may be cause for punishment tomorrow. The ground rules are constantly shifting. In some alcoholic homes, complete chaos erupts.

Roger told of how painful it was to lie in bed at night and listen to his parents fighting in the next room. No matter what he did to shut out the sound of their angry voices, he could not get away from feeling the tension as the arguments escalated. When dishes began to hit the walls, Roger wanted to scream at his parents to stop it. The next morning, he was always amazed to find the kitchen put back together and his parents acting as though nothing had happened. One day he rummaged through the trash to retrieve a piece of broken plate, just to reassure himself that the fight had really happened. There was no continuity in Roger's family. He could never assume that the mood he had last seen in his parents would carry over to the next time he saw them.

This loss of continuity has profound effects on children. CoAs learn to not trust their environment and to be constantly vigilant for signs that the ground rules are being changed. One of the most striking features about the therapy groups I run for ACAs is the failure of what happens in one week's meeting to carry over to the next. It is as though the group members arrive each week and start getting to know each other all over again. Their childhood experiences have evidently taught them not to trust that their relationships will have any continuity. This was exactly the right strategy to use when living with parents whose personalities changed rapidly. But it is not an effective strategy for building intimate relationships.

Respect for Privacy

Healthy families are built on the belief that each member is a separate individual. Without respect for privacy, there is no respect for individuality. Healthy families accept the differences among members as a source of strength for the family as a whole. Privacy is seen as necessary in order for each individual to discover his or her own innate talents. It is also supported as necessary so that people can take adequate care of themselves. Closed doors are knocked on before a room is entered, mail is not opened, and people are allowed to have their private thoughts.

One of the most consistent characteristics of an alcoholic family is the intrusiveness that permeates interactions among members. The alcoholic parent is particularly prone to barging into other people's lives with little regard for whether or not they have been invited. They may burst into a child's bedroom without knocking. They may ask a teenage girl questions about her sexuality, unaware of the nervousness the girl is trying to hide. They may walk into the bathroom and urinate when their teenager is taking a bath. Alcoholic families may keep a lot of secrets, but they know very little about real privacy.

When Tom's father talked, he put his face within inches of Tom's and spoke in a booming voice. Tom felt as though he had been taken hostage; he felt that his physical space had been violated. There is no way to explain these things to a drunk, and Tom simply learned to tolerate the intrusion without showing any reaction. It should come as no surprise that one of Tom's primary problems as an adult is that he feels numb inside whenever he tries to be physically or emotionally intimate with another person. He fears that others will overwhelm him if he lets them get close.

What may feel like playfulness to a drunk parent may be seen by the child as an intrusion into the child's world by an unknowing and unwelcome bully. Tom's father could be uproariously funny, but his humor frequently developed into cruel teasing and then into biting sarcasm, driving Tom's younger sister to tears. An alcoholic parent's efforts to play often turn into demands that their children let them become the center of attention. Whenever Tom's dad came out to play ball with Tom and his friends, he had to be the pitcher. He always dominated any activity he entered.

This lack of respect for privacy stems from the extreme self-centeredness of parents when they are intoxicated, or when they are obsessed by thoughts of an intoxicated spouse. They lose sight of their children as separate individuals. Children become extensions of their parents—little actors who play roles in the adults' drama. They no longer have any autonomy. When children are seen as existing to meet their parents' needs, they have no need for privacy.

Focused Attention

The single concept of focused attention summarizes many of the characteristics seen in healthy families. Children do not need constant attention in order to develop. In fact, constant attention would probably be counterproductive. What children need, and what high-functioning families tend to give, is *focused* attention. This type of attention has two components: schedule and quality.

Schedule   If parents focus attention on two children for the same number of times per day, the fact of when these times occur can still make a profound difference. Schedule A might include times when a child awakens in the middle of the night crying fearfully, when he needs to be fed during the day, when he needs to be changed, when he is most playful and wants someone to share this with, and when he is feeling lonely. Schedule B might include times when the parent has had enough of an eye-opener that he can manage to fix breakfast, when he is intoxicated enough that he is feeling playful and expects the child to join in, when he has finished his ritual two drinks after getting home and is ready to be greeted by his children, and when he is made to feel guilty for how his drunken behavior upset the kids the night before. The timing of the first schedule reflects the child's needs, while the second schedule clearly stems from the parent's needs.

The child-centered and parent-centered schedules for focused attention produce very different worlds for children to grow up in. If care is given to you according to someone else's timing, you learn to control your needs rather than communicate them. You learn that the world cannot be trusted. And you become a reactor to the world, rather than an actor on it. On the other hand, if you receive care more or less at those times when you most need it, you begin developing a trust that the world has your best interests at heart. It begins to make sense for you to be aware of your needs and communicate them. You learn to act on the world, confident that other people will notice and respond to you. The difference between the two schedules is that between living in a cold, hostile universe and living in a friendly, orderly one.

Quality   The quality of attention being focused is also critical. When focused attention is truly present, a person is bringing the full range of human emotional responsiveness to bear. It is through our parents' emotional responses to us that we learn the rules of human interaction. When a child cries, the parent usually shows concern and compassion. When the child smiles, the parent usually smiles back. Human interactions are predictable, by and large, and occur in response to identifiable events.

Alcoholic parents, almost by definition, cannot bring the full range of human emotional responsiveness to bear in interactions with their children. The effects of alcohol on the brain invariably restrict the range of available emotions. Those emotions that do remain are altered by the alcohol. Anger in a sober person and anger in an intoxicated person are not the same emotion. An expression of love from someone who is drunk is just not the same as an expression of love from the same person when sober and aware of what he or she is saying. The quality of attention an alcoholic parent is capable of focusing is not the same as the quality of attention available from a sober parent.

Children have nothing with which to compare their parents' behavior, so they assume that however the parents behave is normal. If the parents are only partially available emotionally, their children's concept of intimate relationships will be crippled. As adults, CoAs may not even know they are missing anything in their relationships, except for having a vague sense of unmet needs deep within.

The effects of your parent's alcoholism on you depend in part on how old you were when family life began being disrupted. Each stage of child development requires the accomplishment of specific tasks. Infants will thus be affected differently—and probably more profoundly—than teenagers.

The task of infancy is to develop a basic trust in the world. In order for a child to develop such trust, the world must respond consistently to an infant's needs. When parental alcoholism creates a chaotic or unresponsive world for them, infants may develop no capacity to trust. In the worst case, there is no bonding between parent and child, leaving the child cut off from being able to connect on an emotional level with other people. Such children may become withdrawn, schizoid, or even psychotic.

Toddlers are involved in the development of independence. Parental alcoholism can disrupt a toddler's growth by providing inconsistent discipline, an excessive emotional charge on issues of impulse control (for example, toilet training), and an unwillingness to allow the child to become separate and autonomous. A child's drive to develop his or her own identity can be badly stunted by alcoholic families.

After the toddler stage, children begin to put energy into mastering their world. There are several destructive ways in which alcoholic parents can relate to their children at this point. They can ignore a child's accomplishments. They can take advantage of accomplishments by making children responsible for their own care as soon as they are capable. Or they can even compete with their children. In all cases, the child's task of feeling comfortable with his or her growing competence will be complicated.

During early adolescence, children are developing an awareness of their own identities. As ironic as it may seem, CoAs frequently feel that their lives are very similar to those of their alcoholic parents—behind a facade of looking normal, they feel very scared and out of control. Without any better models to follow, many CoAs settle for being "pseudoadults," putting their lives on hold until things get better. Rather than continuing to grow emotionally, many CoAs spend the last several years of their life at home simply coping, waiting to get out of their families to begin paying attention to their own lives again.

Finally, during adolescence, the task is to separate from the family enough to stand on one's own. This is extremely difficult for CoAs. Even under the best of circumstances, separation from the family is not easy. When the family as a whole resists losing a child who has been helping to keep things together, the child feels tremendous guilt at the thought of "abandoning" the family. Alcoholic families can greatly prolong—and even prevent—this final task of child development.

Because childhood is a time of such rapid change, it is never possible to predict exactly how a parent's alcoholism will affect a child. Sometimes the effects are quite different on children within the same family, since each child is at a different age when the alcoholism worsens. It is only logical to assume that the damage to a child is more severe the earlier in that child's life parental alcoholism begins to affect the family.

SUMMARY

Our identities crystallize rapidly during early childhood, then continue growing slowly throughout our lives. The deepest and earliest parts lie outside our direct awareness. But, like the core of a crystal, they help form and support the outer, more conscious portions. By the age of six, most children have developed a core sense of self that persists for life.

This process of identity formation is never without flaws. Once the process has been set in motion, it proceeds relentlessly according to a timetable of its own. Under the best of circumstances, people's identities contain many of the dreams and fears that belonged to their parents. There is sufficient time during one's adult life to sort these out and to purify one's own identity until it arises primarily from within.

Children of alcoholics are forced to crystallize their identities under circumstances that are far from optimal. Their environment lacks a core feeling of safety. Communication is distorted by denial, leading to the deafening silence of secrets. Self-care is misinterpreted as selfishness. Roles become rigid so that the family can be protected from change. A sense of continuity does not exist. Neither is there any significant privacy. In the midst of this unhealthy environment, CoAs must pass through the critical stages of developing trust, autonomy, mastery, identity, and the ability to separate themselves from those around them. Their horizons are limited by underlearning at each of these stages of development.

Looking at your family from the vantage point of an adult, without the blinders of denial, is often painful. It is easy to get lost in despair and hopelessness. When this happens, remind yourself that recovery is a road that leads through the dark clouds of pain to the light on the other side.

If the pain is all that you can see at this point, just remember that you are not alone. Others have been through to the other side and have come back to show you the way.

4.

A Time to Feel: Post-traumatic Stress and the ACA

I first became aware of the role stress plays in molding ACAs while working in a veterans' hospital. Many of the characteristics commonly seen in ACAs are also seen in some Vietnam veterans.

Any of us can be wounded psychologically by stress if it is too unrelenting and intense. The most carefully documented examples of people who have been overwhelmed by abnormal levels of stress have been in the case of combat veterans. During the Vietnam era, our understanding of the lasting effects of being in combat underwent further advances. These effects—which had earlier been referred to as battle fatigue and shell shock, among other things—came to be called post-traumatic stress disorder, or PTSD.

Human reactions to stress follow a pattern.* When any event raises more feelings than we can tolerate, we react by quickly entering into denial. If the stress is dealt with in a healthy manner, this denial is interrupted from time to time by the unexpected upwelling of emotions. In effect, we deal with stress with an internal pendulum, which swings freely

---

*A detailed description of reactions to stress can be found in *Stress Response Syndromes* by Mardi Horowitz, M.D. New York: Jason Aronson, Inc., 1976.

back and forth between our denial of these feelings and the intrusion of the feelings into our awareness. As long as the pendulum is free to keep swinging, we eventually resolve the stress without any lasting wound.

PTSD develops when a person's normal coping mechanisms are confronted with abnormal levels of stress, overwhelming that person's ability to break the stress down into digestible bites. The pendulum that is supposed to swing freely either gets stuck in the denial or the intrusive phase or else makes wild swings between the two.

Not all stresses are equally likely to produce PTSD. For example, we know that a prolonged series of traumatic events is more likely to produce PTSD symptoms than a single event. We also know that stresses that are perceived as being of human origin produce more symptoms. Finally, we know that a person is more likely to develop symptoms of PTSD if the trauma is experienced while the person is living in a closed social system, especially one in which reacting to the stress is seen by others as weakness.

In order for PTSD to exist, you must undergo a stress more severe than that ever endured by most people. Everyone agrees that combat experience fits this description. Alcoholic families create many of the same stresses for children as those that exist in combat. CoAs are subjected to continual trauma on a daily basis, and the pain in their lives is inflicted by other people. They are often labeled as weak if they cannot take the stress. Such a situation lies outside the range of what should be considered normal experience.

There are four major symptoms of post-traumatic stress disorder: *reexperiencing of the trauma, psychic numbing, hypervigilance,* and *survivor guilt.* I will discuss each of these symptoms in detail a bit later. But first, the following stories of two ACAs who recently sought therapy from me will serve to illustrate the symptoms of PTSD, including those that on the surface appear to be contradictory.

Deborah

Deborah was thirty-seven years old when she made an appointment with me to explore whether therapy might be useful for her. Her style-conscious appearance and businesslike manner were those of a successful young professional. We were to have, she led me to understand, a doctor-to-doctor discussion about her life.

She sat with her legs wound firmly together, her arms folded, and her eyes looking directly into mine. Everything about her was tightly bound and in control. Even though what she told me about herself left her vulnerable, her voice seemed to drone on and on without any inflection. Never once did spontaneous emotion break through her slow and measured presentation.

Deborah told me that success had not satisfied her deeper needs. She realized that unless she could find a way to become more comfortable with her feelings, she would never find real intimacy or quality in her life. She spoke of fearing intimacy, but she also emphasized her ignorance of how to achieve it in her relationships. She described going numb inside whenever anyone seemed attracted to her. The only time she allowed herself to feel any emotion was when she was helping others with their problems. A tremendous sadness lurked just behind her voice as she told her story.

During childhood, Deborah's family life had been highly structured, predictable, and relatively sterile emotionally. Her father was a successful professor of biochemistry and was devoted to his career. Deborah worshiped him and longed for more of his attention. She saw her mother as a nobody with no education and no activities outside of her household duties. There were no arguments in this home. There was only the family's intense belief that they were a model of rationality and mature behavior.

Only two things tarnished the family's image, and no one outside the house was ever allowed to see either. One of these was that the mother's deep dependence on the father was complicated by periodic bouts of depression, during which Deborah took over most of her mother's family functions. The first episode of depression followed the death of Deborah's mother's own severely alcoholic father. Deborah's father responded to his wife's periodic depression by evincing a sense of disgust. He became even more remote emotionally, and he often chided his wife about her weakness.

The second blemish appeared during Deborah's early teen years, when her father's daily cocktail hour suddenly became an excuse for much heavier drinking. Both his work and his health suffered. When he was diagnosed as having a peptic ulcer and was advised to discontinue alcohol, he decided it was irrational to drink and stopped abruptly. He abstained for the rest of his life, but he entered no treatment or recovery program to help him achieve more comfort with his emotions. Although his work and health quickly recovered, the relationship with his wife became more distant and acrimonious. This was most pronounced during her times of depression, since he felt that she should simply stop her depression in the same matter-of-fact way that he had stopped drinking.

At first, Deborah remembered few specific events from her childhood. All she recalled was feeling like an outsider during high school and college and making up for a lack of relationships by throwing herself into academic studies. During therapy she recalled a bout of panic attacks that had begun when she was eight years old. These attacks usually occurred during the

night. She rarely told anyone about them. On one occasion, when she was ten years old, her baby-sitter had
to call her parents home from a restaurant because of
Deborah's sudden panic at their absence. Little was
ever said about this event by her parents. They simply
went out less often, and the attacks became less frequent.

After college, when it came time to decide on post-
graduate goals, Deborah's father began making plans for
her to enter a doctoral program in biochemistry. Her
panic attacks returned in full force and were accom-
panied by brief, but very deep, depressions. Deborah
"found herself applying to medical schools" without
knowing why, but she did not tell her father that she had
done so until she had been accepted and could surprise
him with the news.

The first two years of medical school were good
times for Deborah. She finally felt free from her family
and its problems. Within six months she had moved in
with a boyfriend and had begun to focus her social life
around their relationship. When she began having direct
contact with patients, she found herself deeply upset by
their suffering. Death began to haunt her. As her emotional turmoil grew, Deborah seriously considered leaving medical school.

She leaned more heavily on her boyfriend for support, but she panicked whenever he sought more intimacy or commitment in their relationship. Their sexual
life plummeted to zero. She began to need continual
reassurance of her worth. Arguments became fierce and
frequent, until finally her boyfriend left her. Deborah
plunged into the deepest depression she had ever
known.

A kindly radiologist near retirement coaxed her
back into her studies. Deborah lost herself in the science

and technology of radiology and wrote a theoretical paper that assured her acceptance in the radiology residency of her choice.

Toward the end of her training Deborah again moved in with a boyfriend. This man drank often, and eventually he stopped hiding how much he drank. Deborah's relationship with him was stormy, and there were many breakups and reconciliations. None of Deborah's colleagues suspected the chaos of her personal life. When her boyfriend was ordered to either enter an alcoholism treatment center or face jail for petty larceny, Deborah dutifully attended the family portions of the treatment program to help his recovery. She was incensed when she was told by the staff that she had problems as well. She put away the books they gave her about children of alcoholics, and she continued to believe that all she had to do was help her friend be stronger.

The push that got Deborah to make an appointment with me came when her friend left her after six months of sobriety. He complained that it was not healthy for him to remain in a relationship with her unless she was seeking recovery from her own problems. Deborah went into a tailspin of panic attacks and suicidal depression. On her birthday, she received a package from her ex-boyfriend—and in it were the ACA books she had put on her shelf without ever opening. That night, she began to read them. What she read shook her so deeply that she began to plan her suicide. Somehow she "found herself on the phone" with me a couple of days later, asking for a meeting. Amazingly, it was in the midst of even this much turmoil and crisis that she sat in my office that first day, tightly composed, wanting to have a doctor-to-doctor discussion about her life.

Alex

Although Alex was forty-one years old, he had the air
of an adolescent, slumping in his chair and treating me
with a mixture of deference and subtle defiance. He
immediately began to spill out his story, mixing current
problems with past memories. On several occasions he
cried openly, then choked back his tears and continued
to tell me rambling fragments of his life. It was difficult
to keep his attention on a single topic. He felt immense
relief at being with me, but he also felt desperate for
practical answers and overwhelmed by all that was happening to him. It was clear that he had much to gain
from therapy, but the first step was to note his impa-
tience, to respect it, and to point out that it represented
the greatest impediment to his healing.

In contrast to Deborah's family, in which a facade
of respectability and predictability was maintained,
Alex's life had been chaotic from the start. His mother
was a diner waitress who periodically left her children
with relatives and went off to Reno on binges. Invariably, during each binge she would enter into a whirlwind
romance, only to be abandoned as soon as she became
pregnant. During her absences, Alex often lived with his
aunt and grandmother, both of whom were severely alcoholic. The grandmother had been married to an alcoholic
bar owner. She had inherited the business after her
husband died (his death had resulted from massive gastrointestinal bleeding while he was passed out on the
stairs leading to their apartment above the bar). She
often told people the story of how she had stepped over
her husband's body after closing the bar that night, too
drunk herself to notice the pool of blood.

Alex remembers neither living situation with any
fondness. When he was with his mother he was treated

to her fantasy world, with its dreams and schemes of catching Mr. Wonderful punctuated by vile outbursts of anger that came without reason or warning. His mother disciplined him by beating him about the abdomen and groin with her fists. She justified these beatings to Alex by telling him that stern discipline was necessary or he would turn out no better than his father (whoever *he* was). Alex first ran away to his grandmother's at the age of six.

Life with his grandmother and aunt was, if anything, even more chaotic. One or the other of them was always married to someone new. Invariably, the new "stepfathers" were alcoholic. Some ignored Alex, while others abused and beat him.

The one advantage of being with his grandmother was that Alex never doubted her love and acceptance. Her home, such as it was, was always open to him. So was her heart, if he could catch her before four in the afternoon, when she usually retired to the bar for the rest of the day. Alex would hurry home from school just to go into the bar and sit next to her. She did not even have to acknowledge his presence; it was enough for him just to be there with her. When Alex ran away to his grandmother's after his mother beat him on his ninth birthday, he arrived only to learn from his aunt that his grandmother had died two months earlier. He still does not know how she died or where she is buried.

Out of embarrassment, Alex never brought any friends into his home. He knew his family was different. Every weekend was a continuous drinking party, with strangers wandering in and out of the apartment, taking showers or scavenging through the refrigerator. Alex dealt with this by being out of the house as much as possible. He joined a gang of boys who experimented with glue sniffing and vandalism, and he eventually

spent one year in a juvenile-detention home. At age
sixteen, Alex ran away and panhandled in San Francisco
for two years. When he got desperate, he worked as a
male prostitute, although he never liked this and always
had to get drunk to tolerate it.

At eighteen, Alex got arrested for shoplifting, and
he joined the army in order to avoid jail. He enjoyed the
tough but fair discipline of the army and considered
making it his career. This became impossible when his
drinking began interfering with his performance. He
was given a medical discharge after he drove an army
truck off the road in a drunken stupor one afternoon. He
suffered several broken ribs and a broken leg in the
accident.

Alex moved back to San Francisco and became a
cabdriver. He drank only after work and on weekends.
Five years later, he met a woman who had recently been
divorced and had little money. The woman had a four-
year-old son, to whom Alex immediately became devoted. Alex moved in with the woman within three days
and began to support her and her son financially. During
the next two years, the woman began working at a local
bank and quickly became secretary to the branch man-
ager. Alex and his girlfriend began attending a local
church regularly. It was through this congregation, and
in response to his girlfriend's wishes, that Alex eventually began to attend AA. At first he experimented with
intermittent drinking, but he quit when his stepson said
he did not like the smell of beer on "daddy's" breath.
Alex remembered what it was like to smell alcohol as a
child.

During the next two years, Alex became increas-
ingly distressed by his relationship with his girlfriend.
He longed to feel closer but felt he could not trust her.
He constantly looked for clues that she was unhappy and

having affairs. He was never able to discuss his fears directly with her. Instead, he found himself getting irritable and criticizing her even when he knew it was not warranted. He was always defensive and often mistook a difference of opinion as criticism.

Above all, he was ruled by fear. He would awaken early in the morning and plan everything he had to do to avoid disaster during that day. He never felt that he could relax and simply enjoy some of the good things that he and his girlfriend had. Fears that it might all be taken away from him or that his inadequacies would ruin things for him constantly intruded into his mind. At times he threatened his girlfriend with violence in order to get their arguing to stop. At the suggestion of his AA sponsor, Alex attended an Al-Anon meeting that had a focus on adult children of alcoholics. In talking to people after the meeting, he learned of the possibility of therapy for dealing with ACA issues and contacted me the following day.

The stories of Deborah and Alex illustrate two opposite personality styles. The first style is that of being overly contained and out of touch with most feelings; the other is that of being at the mercy of whatever feelings happen to well up. And yet both Deborah and Alex are adult children of alcoholics, and being raised in an alcoholic family played a critical role in how each of them experiences the world. As with most opposites in psychology, Deborah's numbness and Alex's sense of being overwhelmed by feelings are two sides of the same coin. It is also not uncommon to see such extremes of numbness and emotional overload alternating in the same person. Both Deborah's numbness and Alex's emotional overload are operating according to the same underlying rules. These rules are dictated by the normal ways in which people react to abnormal levels of stress.

The Four Symptoms of PTSD

Following are some characteristic experiences that can occur within the four major symptoms of post-traumatic stress disorder.

1. Reexperiencing of the Trauma
   Nightmares
   Recurrent, obsessive thoughts
   Sudden reemergence of survival behavior in the face of events that resemble the original trauma
   Emotional overload
2. Psychic Numbing
   A sense of depersonalization
   Not fitting into one's surroundings
   A feeling of emotional anesthesia
   Constriction of emotions, especially in situations demanding intimacy, tenderness, or sexuality
3. Hypervigilance
   Inability to relax
   Frequent startle response
   Chronic anxiety
   Panic attacks
4. Survivor Guilt
   Chronic depression
   Sourceless sense of guilt

If you recognize more than one of these characteristics in yourself, it is very likely that you experienced significant stress as a child, whether you remember it or not.

The four symptoms of PTSD are known to occur at any age. They do not necessarily appear at the time the stress is present. Rather, they are the long-term effects of the extraordinary coping strategies required to survive the stress. These symptoms are the scars left from the very deep wounds inflicted by overwhelming stress. In many cases, the symptoms increase with age, as one's adaptive capacity and physical stamina decline or as more and more chronic stress is accumulated.

Most veterans, and most CoAs, assume that these symptoms will heal with the passage of time. However, time alone is incapable of healing such wounds. We all want to believe that just because our intellect can no longer remember events from our past, our emotions must also no longer be affected. This is not the case. Every therapist has seen many clients who are suddenly surprised by the intensity of their emotional reactions to events that occurred fifty or more years ago.

The symptoms of PTSD continue to exist until an active process of healing occurs. We will look more closely at this process in later chapters on recovery and treatment. For the moment, it is important to look directly at the wounds themselves and at the events that caused them. The first step in any healing process is the acknowledgment of the full reality of the wounds.

Reexperiencing the Trauma

Alex is a striking example of someone for whom the stress pendulum has stuck in the intrusive phase. Feelings are constantly threatening to rise up and overwhelm him. The original trauma of being abandoned has left him with an intense reaction to the slightest hint that he might be left by his girlfriend. In a sense, the feelings of the original trauma are reexperienced over and over whenever anything even vaguely resembling it occurs in Alex's life. He is at the mercy of anything that might trigger this intense emotional reaction, and he reacts to it by trying to discharge his feelings as quickly as possible in order to feel less vulnerable.

Examples of reexperiencing the trauma include the following:

- Immediate anger (sadness or other intense emotions) when around someone who is intoxicated.
- Fear response to someone's anger at you, or at the prospect of losing a relationship—even temporarily.
- Extreme defensiveness when criticized.
- Startle responses to small events that preceded arguments when you were a youngster.

Among Vietnam veterans, this symptom has taken several forms. Actually, it is a cluster of related symptoms. After returning to civilian life, many veterans complained of having recurrent and intrusive thoughts, images, and feelings of their Vietnam experience. Veterans often train themselves not to pay direct attention to these intrusions when they occur. Unfortunately, since it is impossible to control what one pays attention to during sleep, recurrent nightmares of combat experience are common.

One client of mine spoke of not remembering a single day in the twelve years since he had been discharged from the service when the word *Vietnam* did not flash through his thoughts at least once. Despite his wanting to forget that time in his life, it continued to intrude unbidden into his awareness. His combat experience had been so painful that his ability to comprehend and integrate the stress was overwhelmed. A permanent emotional charge was attached to the thoughts and images of Vietnam that filled his mind.

Perhaps the most dramatic form this symptom takes is the sudden reemergence of a whole pattern of feelings, thoughts, and behavior in response to situations that are similar to the original event. A veteran may be walking down the street and unexpectedly have a firecracker explode, or a car backfire, right next to him. Instantly, his heart races and his palms perspire; he dives to the pavement, searching urgently for the source of the incoming fire. At the moment of being overwhelmed by the danger in Vietnam, a new reflex was born. Clearly, such behavior did have real survival value during combat. But today it has become an inappropriate automatic reflex.

A joke among ACAs demonstrates a similar phenomenon: "Alcoholic parents never die; they just lie six feet under the ground and wait for you." This poignantly expresses the sense that there seems to be no escape from reexperiencing the trauma. Many have moved 2,000 miles away from their families, only to discover that their recurrent, obsessive thoughts about how things are going at home continue unabated. One ACA who has not seen his mother for several years owns a telephone-answering machine for the express purpose of being able to monitor incoming calls in case she tries to intrude into his life again. Emotional detachment from an alcoholic family seems to be considerably harder than physical detachment, and it is often far more difficult for an ACA to leave home emotionally than it is for a non-ACA.

The most direct parallel between ACAs and Vietnam veterans involves the suddenness with which survival behavior can reemerge in response to events that symbolically resemble the original traumatic situation. A particularly dramatic example is provided by the story of Pat, the head nurse in an intensive-care unit. Still in her late twenties, Pat was highly regarded for her competence, responsibility, and sense of professionalism. She entered therapy because of her concern about the widening gap between how others perceived her and how she saw herself. Outwardly, she projected a strength that calmed those around her and gave them confidence that she could handle anything. Inwardly, Pat felt an increasing sense of chaos. She was convinced that she was only pulling the wool over people's eyes; she lived with a constant dread of impending catastrophe. The more competent she looked, the less sure of herself she felt inside.

During the course of the therapy, Pat received a call from her daughter's school, informing her that the child had a mild fever. In order to get her daughter home, Pat needed to leave work two hours early. She arranged for someone to cover her duties for the remainder of her shift, then double-checked to be sure that all the doctors' orders had been followed and that the patients were stable. Assured that she was not leaving any stones unturned, Pat began walking the twenty feet to her supervisor's office to let the woman know she was leaving. By the time she stood before her supervisor, her heart was pounding and her palms were sweating. She felt light-headed and on the verge of panic. She felt guilty for asking others to take over two hours of her duties, and she was convinced that her supervisor would see her as irresponsible. By the time she began to speak, she found herself rocking back and forth from foot to foot, and her voice cracked with emotion.

I asked Pat to allow the emotions that had been present when she stood in front of her supervisor to return to her awareness. After she had developed a detailed memory of these feelings, I asked how old she felt. Pat immediately said, "Six years old." When I asked her to tell me about her life at six, the third thing she mentioned was that this was when her father's alcoholism first got out of control. Pat remembered how she learned to stop bothering him with her needs and to hide her feelings in order to protect herself from his arbitrary outbursts of anger.

For Pat, the symbolic equivalent was having to go to an authority figure for help when her own needs prevented her from discharging her usual responsibilities. Pat had long ago found this to be a dangerous thing to do; people learn by experience. By being extremely competent and responsible, Pat usually avoided having to ask other people for help. By being obsessively organized, she made sure that her personal needs rarely intruded on her responsibilities.

Her experience as a child told her that authority figures could not be counted on to validate her needs or to respect her best efforts when she was unable to fulfill every commitment. Whenever she was forced as an adult into a vulnerable situation with authority figures, the past reemerged with a vengeance and seemed to take over for the moment. By exploring her reactions to this event, we were able to deepen her understanding of what it had really felt like for her to be a child. She eventually found herself having a new kind of empathy for the fate that had been dealt her years ago.

Pat's story is only one example drawn from thousands. ACAs frequently speak of spending two years in therapy, only to go home for Thanksgiving and find themselves acting in all their old self-destructive ways within ten seconds of entering the house. Despite your firm resolutions to speak openly about feelings, you may find that the old rules reassert themselves and make it impossible to open the conversation. Feelings of sadness or anger may be triggered by something as simple as the sound of ice clinking in a glass. Massive displays of defensiveness often take over your behavior whenever there is a hint of your being attacked, criticized, or just disagreed with.

I have watched an ACA rock back and forth in his chair, unable to speak without crying, every time someone leaves his therapy group. This is a clear example of reexperiencing the trauma. This individual tells of having been raised by two alcoholic parents who went on binges together and failed to return home at least once a week. And this was when he was only three years old.

When I saw Alex in therapy, he was in a state of reexperiencing the trauma almost constantly. The experiences of having been repeatedly abandoned by his mother and, especially, of having lost his grandmother without ever being told that she had died had had such a pervasive and overwhelming impact on his early life that the normal psychological mechanisms for dealing with stress were totally inadequate. He was repeatedly flooded with intolerable levels of fear. His primary way of escaping from this fear was by manipulating himself biochemically. By adding chemicals such as alcohol and marijuana to his brain, he was able to decommission the neurological circuits producing fear and anxiety. However, when he began abstaining from drugs and alcohol, he gradually returned to a perpetual state of reexperiencing his abandonment fears. If his girlfriend raised an eyebrow at the wrong time, if she came home late, if she came home early—any of this recalled for him the feeling that whatever he had could be taken from him without a moment's notice. The stress pendulum was stuck in the intrusive phase.

Psychic Numbing

Vietnam veterans frequently became aware, after returning home, of feeling estranged and detached from the world around them. For many, it made sense to blame these feelings on changes that had happened in this country during the time they were serving in Vietnam. But this feeling of not fitting in was too pervasive to be just a sense that the country had changed. Many veterans also found that they were uncomfortable in their old communities, their old jobs, or even their own families. When this was explored in therapy, it became clear that many no longer "fit in" their own emotions in the way they had before their combat experience. It was as though a wall of cotton existed between themselves and their feelings. Apparently, the basic relationship that existed between these veterans and their emotional world had been somehow altered. The following are examples of psychic numbing:

- Having no feelings during times of stress.
- Suddenly experiencing a "wall" between yourself and your feelings.
- Being "confused" instead of having feelings.
- Just having a lump in your throat instead of allowing feelings to emerge.
- Fearing that feelings will overwhelm you if they begin to be shown.

This numbing and constriction of emotions is particularly apparent in circumstances that demand intimacy, tenderness, or sexuality. Although they might crave intimacy, PTSD sufferers report that they become emotionally vacant whenever someone is willing to establish intimate contact with them. Emotional anesthesia leaves them unaware of what their feelings are precisely when it is most important to be in direct touch with them.

Deborah, whose story was told earlier in this chapter, is a good example of how the development of psychic numbing during childhood can create a legacy that reaches throughout the adult years. She had become so numbed to her feelings that she could eloquently describe how the quality of her life was being destroyed by her fear of intimacy, and yet she could say this without any apparent emotional reaction to her own fate. I remember her halting comment that "I sometimes have the fear . . . I am achieving . . . everything I could possibly hope to professionally, . . . and yet it is clear . . . that the essential core . . . of what it means to be human . . . is completely beyond my grasp."

Psychic numbing is so common among CoAs that it is seen as normal. It seems inconceivable to most ACAs that everyone does not feel the same way. Psychic numbing is an inherent psychological mechanism that is naturally activated during times of overwhelming stress. It is especially likely to occur if action is required in order to survive the danger. The following story illustrates how psychic numbing develops and why it can be a useful coping strategy at times.

Luke

At the time he was drafted into the Vietnam war, Luke was nineteen years old and had drifted aimlessly since graduating from high school. Basic training seemed like twenty-four-hour football practice. Luke got into the best shape he had ever been in, and he enjoyed the male camaraderie surrounding him day and night. Special training in artillery gave him a sense of responsibility and competence that went beyond anything he had ever felt. After arriving in Vietnam, he began to feel some anxiety, but the experience of being treated as an adult for the first time in his life was still very positive.

All this changed in the blinding fire and thunder of an instant, when an incoming shell exploded only yards away. Luke had been protected from shrapnel and the full force of the explosion by a wall of sandbags. When he looked over the wall, he saw his best buddy gurgling to death on his own blood. A piece of shrapnel had ripped through his neck and severed his windpipe. To this day, Luke has an extremely vivid recollection of the smell and sounds of that moment. Witnesses of trauma to others frequently report such lucid memories of the original scene.

Luke recalled in therapy what happened inside himself at that moment. He described how his feelings about his dying friend were suddenly put away into the back of his mind and he was able to swing into action. It was as though there had literally been a gulf that had opened up between himself and a part of his experience. A rupture was created between Luke and his emotions. Lying within each of us is the potential for creating such a rupture in the face of extremely traumatic events. This potential lies within us because it has concrete survival value. Those people who are capable of performing such a protective act are the ones who more often survive severe trauma. However, these emotions need to be taken out later and dealt with; otherwise, they fester beneath the psychic numbing.

It takes no imagination to understand why CoAs who were physically or sexually abused experience a rupture between themselves and their experience. Becoming numb is the last line of defense against being totally overwhelmed. When children are unable to get a parent to stop beating them, they can at least turn off what they are feeling.

Actual loss of control over one's physical safety at the hands of a parent can irrevocably change a person's relationship to the world. No amount of new perspective gained as an adult can help a person to reclaim the degree of control over his or her destiny that appeared to exist before the violence.

It is harder for people to understand how psychic numbing can occur in ACAs who have no history of overt physical abuse. The explanation for the numbing in these cases is the unrelenting covert abuse—for example, the lack of focused attention—that can occur in even the most politely alcoholic family. The following memory was related by the son of an anesthesiologist. Tom's father never experienced professional difficulties from his alcoholism, despite his daily habit of stopping for a drink on the way home from the hospital and having two quick cocktails as soon as he arrived. When he was off duty, he drank between one and two six-packs of beer—to quench his thirst, he said.

Tom

One day, when Tom was nine years old, his father called him out to the barn to help plow the field. His dad was off duty for the weekend, and this usually meant that the drinking started by mid-morning. Tom felt uncomfortable as his father talked to him, because he tended to stand very close when he was intoxicated. Tom looked at the slightly bloated, ruddy face looming over him and felt a constant urge to back away. But he stood his ground and hid his discomfort in order not to upset his father.

It made no sense to try to plow the field that day, since they had gotten the tractor stuck in the muddy soil the day before and it had rained again last night. As his father explained why they would be more successful today, Tom felt as if he were being held hostage. He knew that his father had already tried to convince his mother that the field could be plowed, and she had told him he was crazy. Tom was caught between the two. If he agreed with his father, his mother would think he was crazy too. But if he answered his father truthfully, he would be seen as siding with his mother. It was a no-win situation.

Tom immediately went into his detached survival behavior. He knew that arguing rationally with his father would only add fuel to the fire, and he would have to stand there with his father's face looming over him for the next forty minutes. If he agreed with his father, however, he would be able to get out of there in only thirty minutes—but he'd also have to go out and struggle with the stuck tractor again. Since any hostage's primary goal is to escape captivity, Tom practiced one of the skills described by Huckleberry Finn. He allowed his father to see in him whatever he needed to: he nodded a little bit when his father wanted him to, he smiled a little bit when it was required, but he never really responded enough to encourage his dad. This required a delicate balance, but Tom had begun to master this. As Tom now explains, he emptied himself by putting his own feelings out of his mind. This permitted him to focus all his attention on responding in the way his father required, but in small enough doses so that talking to Tom soon proved unsatisfying. The result was that he got out of there in fifteen minutes!

Tom completes this picture by adding that, when he closes his eyes and calls up a picture of the scene, he literally sees the back of his own head in front of his father's face. In order for him to behave as he did under such circumstances, Tom had to distance himself emotionally as much as possible. He had learned how to foster the gap that could open up between himself and his experience. He had learned how to place his own feelings on the other side of this gap, and then to widen the gulf until they were distant enough that he was able to focus most of his attention on his father, and what his father's needs were, rather than on his own needs. A flood of tears came to Tom's eyes when he first recalled this scene in my office.

Let's pause for a moment and look at this scene from another perspective. Imagine yourself as a neighbor. As you pull out of your driveway and pass by the above scene, you see what looks like an ideal relationship. The father is out by the tractor with his son, discussing something about the field. From all outward appearances, there is little to indicate the extraordinary psychological mechanisms churning within Tom. Quiet desperation is easy to miss, precisely because it is so quiet. We become aware of it in the above scene only if we look at what is happening through Tom's eyes.

In order to interpret Tom's experience accurately, it is imperative to remember that the above scene is not an isolated incident. For most children of alcoholics, the experience of being hostage to an adult's alcoholism pervades their entire childhood. Relating to such a world without learning to numb yourself is simply too painful.

Children who develop psychic numbing grow up to be adults who have no empathy for their own fate. They feel more for the fates of other people, and frequently of children, than they do for themselves and their own childhoods. *Once this lack of empathy for oneself is established, the child within is doomed to remain a hostage for life unless the road to recovery is discovered.*

Deborah demonstrated another facet of psychic numbing

during therapy. She often suddenly became "unavailable," as though she had faded off into the distance and had broken direct contact on any meaningful level. She developed a glazed look in her eyes, although she never broke eye contact with me when this occurred. Others might break eye contact, look upward, start breathing more shallowly, or develop more rigidity in their facial expressions. You may be aware of how you manipulate your attention at a moment's notice to avoid upwelling feelings or uncomfortable levels of intimacy. This process has many names. Some describe it as the "wall coming up." Others say they "phase out," "go into the ozone," "blank out," or "get confused."

When I asked Deborah where she had gone during these episodes, she would only answer that she had gone "away." Eventually in the therapy she became more sensitive to when she was doing this, and she would let me know it was happening without my having to notice it first. When she acknowledged that her distancing from me did not occur at random but was always in response to something she was trying to avoid, she was able to use this feeling as a sure sign that her denial was active. Her willingness to become sensitive to her psychic numbing and to use it in this way was an important step in her recovery process.

Hypervigilance

A third symptom of post-traumatic stress disorder is hypervigilance, or hyperalertness. For a soldier in combat, being fully alert is a necessity from the standpoint of sheer survival. After returning home, many Vietnam veterans found that they were stuck in a state of constant preparation for catastrophe. Their attention had become stuck on automatic pilot, leaving them ceaselessly scanning the environment for hidden dangers, unable to trust that any place would ever be safe again. They were plagued by persistent anxiety, a tendency to startle easily, and an inability to relax long after the trauma of combat had ended. Examples of hypervigilance include these:

- Constantly checking to be sure that other people have done their jobs correctly.
- Assuming that anything that goes wrong is the first sign of a catastrophe.
- Keeping lists in your head of all the things that have to be done before you can relax.
- Constantly feeling that there is something you ought to be doing.

Hyperalertness can also lead to a host of stress-related physical illnesses, such as hypertension, migraine headaches, and gastrointestinal ailments. We can deny the toll that chronic tension takes on us mentally and spiritually, but we cannot fool the body. It will gradually succumb to the excessive wear and tear of being continually tense and ready for action.

If you are a child of an alcoholic, you know what it means to remain ever vigilant for the first signs of danger. ACAs often talk about having extremely sensitive antennae, with which they are constantly checking the world around them. If one person in a crowd raises his eyebrows and looks disapproving, ACAs are likely to notice it immediately and to find themselves reacting to what they think the person might do next.

Hyperalertness is the normal human response to situations that generate a lot of anxiety, and alcoholic families are extremely powerful sources of anxiety for children. You grew up with people whose moods changed rapidly and without explanation. Because the drinking was often hidden, or because as a young child you may not have made the connection between the drinking and changes in your parents' behavior, it was impossible to predict from one moment to the next what your parents were going to do. With the rules constantly changing and the normal ebb and flow of family life destroyed by your parents' drinking, you learned that the only way to keep safe was to become hyperalert to your surrounding world. The sooner you noticed that danger was brewing, the sooner you could get out of the house, start placating your parent, or hide under the bed.

It is important to realize that arbitrary changes in mood happen with both parents, not just with the alcoholic. Your mother might be in a good mood while she is preparing dinner. Suddenly, after a hushed phone call, her mood becomes brooding. She is more distant. You are left without any explanation for this change and probably begin to wonder whether you have done something to produce your mother's sullen withdrawal. The missing information is that your father has called to provide a lame excuse for not being home in time for dinner. Your mother recognized this for what it was—an attempt to cover up for being intoxicated—but she tried to hide his behavior from you.

Behavioral scientists have demonstrated that the most effective way to produce anxiety is to reward and punish an animal arbitrarily. Laboratory rats have developed ulcers when they were rewarded just often enough to think they had figured out the system, only to be punished the next time.

Alex's life with his mother was similarly arbitrary. He could never predict whether her response to the alcohol would be joviality, moroseness, or some other mood. However, once she entered one of these moods, she remained in it no matter what happened around her. Alex remembered falling one day, getting grass stains on his new jeans and cutting his hand. His mother, who was in a jovial mood at the time, laughed off the stains as youthful exuberance. While cleaning up Alex's cut, she told a humorous story of how she had torn the pocket on her new Sunday dress the first time she had worn it. The next day, now in a morose mood, she barked at Alex for still wearing the same dirty jeans. In alcoholic families, there is very little consistency.

Tom told a poignant story about how hypervigilant he had been as a child. He had received his first perfect mark on a spelling test as a third-grader. He remembers running and dancing his way home, still clutching the paper in his hand. As he raced up the porch steps and reached for the doorknob, he felt a sudden damper on his enthusiasm. Instead of bursting into the house, he opened the door sedately and walked into the living room without showing any sign of his excitement. Almost instinctively, he was aware that it was not safe to be exuberant. His father was sitting in the overstuffed chair near the television, reading the evening paper. When his father was sitting in the overstuffed chair near the television and reading the paper at this time of the afternoon, it usually meant that an argument was brewing.

Tom walked past his father, concentrating on whether he was going to make it uninterrupted or whether his father was going to take him hostage. The paper stayed still, and Tom knew that he could move through to the kitchen and probably not get into trouble for failing to greet his father. As soon as he got into the kitchen, he immediately sized up the situation further. His mother seemed relatively happy; no argument had broken out yet. Then, as if it were possible, Tom tried to regain some of the spontaneous pleasure he had felt about his perfect mark on the spelling test. He jumped up and down, waving the paper. "I got 100!" he yelled (but not too loudly, so that he wouldn't disturb his father). Tom remembers that his mother entered into the excitement with him, and together they convinced themselves that it is possible to control your spontaneity without losing any of its real sparkle.

When they cannot predict on the basis of previous events how their parents are going to react to them, most children give up trying to learn the rules of human relationships. It becomes more effective to develop a keen sense of observation. By becoming hypervigilant, a CoA learns to *react* to the world rather than to interact with it.

Although you may have learned how to survive in an

untrustworthy world, the price you pay for having become hyperalert is heavy. It leaves little room for play or for your own feelings, since you are constantly involved in monitoring other people. It never allows you to relax. It is not surprising that many CoAs enter adulthood with a legacy of anxiety and a chronic sense of impending doom. And it is not surprising that ACAs report that difficulty with relationships is their number-one problem. Hypervigilance erodes the foundation of truly intimate relationships by eroding the capacity for trust on which such relationships must be built.

Survivor Guilt

The survivors of fatal disasters often feel obsessively guilty. The question of why they survived, while others perished, can haunt them for years. It does not matter that this guilt is irrational. It is nonetheless real, and it can keep eating away inside a person until help is found. Examples of survivor guilt include the following:

- Feeling callous if you do not help people who say they need you (even if their problems are of their own making).
- Restraining yourself from feeling complete joy.
- Finding some way that you might be responsible for other people's unhappiness and misfortune.
- Refusing to leave relationships and situations that are unhealthy for you in order to avoid feeling guilty.

Many Vietnam veterans suffer agonizing guilt for having survived when so many of their buddies did not. For some, this guilt takes the form of depression. For others, it simply remains a dark cloud that shadows moments when they could be enjoying life to the fullest. Veterans with PTSD even report feeling obligated to rein in their own happiness; to do otherwise feels like a betrayal of those who did not return.

Many veterans are tormented by the question of why they survived and others died or by thoughts of what they might have done to save a buddy's life. It is as though the psyche cannot tolerate acknowledging how utterly powerless we are over life's worst tragedies. It seems absurd to say that life-and-death events revolve around nothing more meaningful than blind luck. Such a universe feels terribly impersonal.

Children of alcoholics can be similarly obsessed with guilt for having survived their families emotionally when other members did not. As noted earlier, many alcoholic families have an unspoken rule that no one is permitted to get any healthier than the sickest member. Therefore, if you have made it out of your family and are establishing an independent life, you may find yourself plagued by a feeling that your very success is a sign of callousness toward family members who are still embroiled in the disease.

This feeling is especially common among ACAs who are the oldest children in their families. These ACAs feel tremendous guilt for having set off on their own, leaving younger brothers and sisters to fend for themselves. Often, the oldest child knows that he or she has been protecting the others up until that time. In addition, the progressive nature of alcoholism might mean that the worst years could still be in store for the family. Naturally, oldest children wonder what right they have to go off and enjoy themselves.

A catch-22 exists for ACAs: the more completely they are able to establish a separate life, the more they feel pulled to return to the family and try one more time to "fix things." One ACA told of his anguish when his parents called to ask for a "loan" of $500 to pay the rent. He knew that they would probably be evicted unless he sent the money. He also knew that he had been planning to use that $500 to take a vacation for the first time in three years. His dilemma came from a history of having sent similar amounts of money to rescue his parents from their latest crisis, only to learn that they had drunk the money away and been evicted anyway. He felt that his only two choices were between keeping the money for his vacation and feeling guilty, or sending the money to his parents and feeling resentment when they squandered it again.

John

John, an oldest child, was groomed from the beginning to shoulder responsibility without complaint. When his father required a medical leave of absence from his corporate executive position to be treated for alcoholism at an out-of-state treatment center, John became the mainstay of the family. He saw his mother as frail and overly dependent on his father, so he felt it was his responsibility to take care of her. John enjoyed his new role as man of the house and fondly remembers the close contact he had with his mother during these times.

By the time John was in his mid-thirties he had built a successful brokerage firm, but he was suffocating under the burden of having become a "big brother" to all of his employees. While his acting this way gave the firm a family feeling, John again found himself in the position of shouldering the responsibility for everyone else's problems. At this point, his father was hospitalized after suffering a seizure. John rushed to his mother's aid once again, but he felt devastated and betrayed when the doctor told him that his father had secretly been abusing sleeping pills ever since he had stopped drinking. As soon as his father was back on his feet, John sold his brokerage firm and moved 2,000 miles away.

Although John established a successful new firm in San Francisco, he lived an essentially transient lifestyle. His small apartment was never fully decorated, and some possessions had still not been taken out of their moving boxes after eight years. He frequently flew back home to help the family with crises. When his father relapsed into his sleeping-pill habit shortly after retiring from his company, John returned home for two months to take care of his mother. As a consequence, his own business suffered substantially. But John could not free himself from what felt like an obligation to shoulder his family responsibilities.

After a year of group therapy, John's father relapsed into pill usage again. John had just bought a house, and his business was at a critical point in its expansion. With the group's support, he called home and said that he would be unable to return immediately. Following this, he was tormented by nightmares of his being an ungrateful son and of scenes of his family's suffering. To his surprise, when he called home again he was told that his younger brother had moved in with his mother temporarily and that everything was being well taken care of. John called his younger brother and was shocked to hear him say all the things that John had secretly felt over the years. John's brother felt compelled to take care of his mother, whom he saw as frail and dependent. Although the younger brother felt trapped, he could not imagine refusing to be responsible for her. He would feel too guilty!

John's story illustrates the exaggerated feelings of guilt and responsibility that ACAs can carry around. John had assumed that his mother would fall apart if he failed to take care of her. The first time he tested this reality, however, his mother easily found someone else to help her. John had never been as indispensable as he had thought, and therein lies the other side of the coin called guilt.

In feeling guilty when they do not rescue their families,

ACAs maintain a sense of importance. It is hard, if not impossible, to give up our need to be important to a parent. Survivor guilt keeps us prisoner to that need and measures our importance to a parent by whether or not that parent recovers.

THROUGH THE EYES OF A CHILD

Being subjected to combat in Vietnam and being held hostage in an alcoholic home as a child are both stressful enough to create symptoms of post-traumatic stress disorder. Luke, the Vietnam veteran, continues to have vivid images of the smells and sounds he experienced as he knelt next to his buddy and saw his shredded windpipe filling with blood. You may have vivid images of the smells and the sounds you experienced as you knelt next to a drunk parent in the middle of the living-room floor, listening carefully to his breathing, wondering if he were still alive. You may have covered your parent with a blanket and sat there shivering with fear while you waited for someone else to come home. The degree of stress CoAs experience must be understood through the eyes of a child, not just through the eyes of an adult.

The deepest wounds often come not just from the trauma of having lived in chaotic and violent conditions but also from having been taken hostage and held in captivity. Such wounds are seen in veterans who were prisoners of war and in CoAs who were physically or sexually abused. Once a soldier has been completely isolated from his comrades, a whole new level of his personality is traumatized. There is no longer anyone around him who can validate his experience. His own emotional reactions to the situation are called into question in a way that can eventually warp his loyalties to the point at which he begins to feel himself empathize with his captors; he may begin to "identify with the aggressor."

In a similar manner, the more abused a child has been, the more likely he or she is to believe that the abuse was deserved. Children have been known to apologize to an abusing parent even as they are being rushed into surgery because of internal injuries resulting from a savage beating. Although this may at first appear incomprehensible, child therapists have been able to untangle the logic that children unconsciously follow in taking the blame for being abused. Understanding this logic is vital not only for those ACAs who have been overtly abused as children, but also for those who have developed any of the symptoms of PTSD through chronic exposure to more covert abuse.

No child has ever done anything horrible enough to deserve to be physically or sexually abused. When such abuse occurs, the child is overwhelmed by emotion and struggles desperately to discover meaning in what is happening. If the abuse is seen realistically, children recognize their innocence and the unfairness of being held hostage to the cruel wishes of someone who is many times larger and stronger and upon whom they are deeply dependent. In simplistic childhood terms, such children see themselves as Saints living in a world of Sinners.

Although such a view of the abuse has some truth, it creates severe problems for a child. What can the child possibly do in such a situation to change what is happening? The abuser is overwhelmingly superior in strength and could never be forced to stop. Children are too small and dependent to remove themselves physically from the setting. And no amount of being good can possibly influence matters, creating a profound sense of impotence and hopelessness. Children without hope fail to thrive. They begin to withdraw energy from the business of growing up. They slow down, or stop, developing. They become apathetic, and they may even die.

Fortunately, nature has given people an adaptive mechanism that helps them to deal with damage of this magnitude. This mechanism sacrifices a realistic view of what is occurring in return for an increased chance of survival. Children spontaneously begin to see themselves as Sinners living in a world of Saints. A heavy price is paid for accepting this distorted perspective. It brings you shame when others mistreat you, and it fosters the feeling that you are responsible for how others are behaving toward you.

However, this distortion also has great value, for it creates a sense of hope. If you are causing the abuse, then at least you have some power. Not only is there an illusion of having power, but there is also the hope that you will eventually learn how to use that power to improve things. This hope can spur you on to rush through the stages of child development, trying to master life's tasks and mature as quickly as possible. Hope, although bought at the expense of a realistic view of the world, is nevertheless worth the price. It is better to survive traumatic events than to be overcome by them. You can deal later on with the repercussions of what you had to do to survive.

Children who remain aware that the abuse they are receiving is undeserved are more likely to fall into apathy and become casualties while still young. Or, they may begin to strike out at the world with such fury that they become perceived by everyone else as the problem. Many youths who come in contact with the juvenile justice system are badly abused CoAs. Their anger is directed at the world, as perhaps it should be. But the world does not tolerate their angry behavior and punishes them for it. Often, those CoAs who had the most realistic perceptions about what was happening in their families are those who enter adulthood with the most strikes against them because of the anger they have acted out and because of their failure to obtain the education needed to succeed in the adult world.

On the other hand, their brothers and sisters who fled from reality still have hope. They have used their anger to spur themselves on to earning many of the tickets, such as college degrees, that are needed to navigate through the adult world. What they so often fail to do, however, is come to terms with the illusion that sustained them throughout their childhood. To relinquish the illusion that their parent is a Saint is just as wrenching as losing a body part. The inevitable reaction is grief.

The reward for relinquishing this illusion is a more solid foundation for your sense of self-worth. As an adult child of an alcoholic, gaining knowledge of the disease aspects of alcoholism can help you to temper your moral judgments of your parents. As adult children of alcoholics, it is possible to move beyond the simplistic view of the world as being made up of either Saints or Sinners.

The use of post-traumatic stress disorder as a framework for understanding many of the characteristics of ACAs has major implications for both our society and for the individual. While society openly acknowledges the devastating effects of alcoholism on the alcoholic, we have forgotten its effects on children. It is time to seriously consider the fate of every child living in an alcoholic home. The evidence is clear, if we are willing to look at it, that the devastation of alcoholism spills over onto every member of the family, especially the very young.

In its charter statement, the National Association for Children of Alcoholics asserts the right of all children to grow up in a safe environment. Once we look more closely at the degree of stress that parental alcoholism generates for children, it should become clear that society has a stake in actively guaranteeing the right of its children to live their lives in relative safety. Suspicion that a child is living in an alcoholic family should become tantamount to suspicion that a child's right to a safe environment is being violated.

For the individual CoA, the framework of PTSD implies that the road to recovery is a lengthy process. You may have very few memories of your childhood. This makes it difficult for you to be realistic about what your experience as a child was. The most effective approach to such lost memories is to use the metaphor "Where there's smoke, there's fire." If you see symptoms in yourself of reexperiencing the trauma, psychic numbing, hypervigilance, or survival guilt, then it is prudent to assume that many of the memories you have lost are of stressful and difficult times. It is not necessary to assume that there was overt abuse in order for you to acknowledge the wounds from your past. The next chapter will help you to explore the ways in which alcoholic families compound whatever wounds occur by ignoring them, which further intensifies the symptoms of post-traumatic stress disorder.

5.

A Time to Separate:
Codependence and the ACA

The characteristics commonly seen in ACAs are of two types. While the first set of characteristics, outlined in the previous chapter, is stress related, the second set is made up of the self-defeating strategies that alcoholic families use to cope with their problems. These strategies, which together are called codependence, attack the personality and sense of self of every family member.

The word *codependence* comes from the term *co-alcoholic,* which refers to spouses who share many of the personality characteristics of their alcoholic husbands or wives. They are like the alcoholic in almost every way, except that they do not drink excessively. When the general term *chemical dependence* began being used to stress the fact that alcohol is as much a drug as cocaine or heroin, the term *co-alcoholism* was changed to *codependence.*

You may not find *codependence* in the dictionary yet.* The word *dependence* is defined as "being influenced or controlled by something else," and the prefix *co-* means "mutu-

---

*The concept of codependence is so new that it still suffers from having no set definition. In a book for professionals entitled *Diagnosing and Treating Codependency: A Guide for Professionals* (Minneapolis: Johnson Institute Books, 1986), I have proposed specific criteria for deciding whether a person is codependent. For those with a clinical interest, these criteria are listed in Appendix IV.

ally." When the two words are combined, they suggest a person who is dependent on and controlled by others who are themselves dependent on or controlled by forces such as alcoholism, compulsive behavior, or chronic illness. The prototypical example would be someone who sacrifices his or her own needs to accommodate an alcoholic spouse whose life is out of control.

Codependent strategies are self-defeating. Although they appear to work initially, their seeds of destruction are built in. If they begin to fail, they can be made to appear to work again if they are attempted with renewed energy. But ultimately they always fail. Codependents are driven by the firm belief that these strategies fail because of their own personal inadequacies, and they base much of their self-esteem on their ability to get these solutions to work. The strategy itself is never questioned. It simply needs to be tried harder, refined more, or timed better to get it to work. In the Al-Anon program this is called "forcing solutions."

Codependence is so devastating because it leads CoAs to ignore the wounds they have suffered. The codependent's strategy for coping with life's problems is to keep quiet about them, as though ignoring their existence will minimize their importance. This is precisely the tactic taken by active alcoholics, and the result is the same for the codependent: the problems continue to worsen, while you become progressively less aware of the real source of your pain.

Codependence is especially crippling for CoAs who have never been exposed to other ways of living. It can lead to their having no knowledge of how to form satisfying relationships with friends, spouses, and even their own children. Too many ACAs enter into multiple marriages, each starting with great promise but in all of which true intimacy fails to develop. Codependence causes ACAs to become increasingly less aware of who they are as they try harder to please others.

Codependence can take on many appearances depending

Common Signs of Codependence

- Excessive pride in self-control.
- Basing self-esteem on getting others to be in a relationship with you.
- Feeling responsible for meeting other people's needs even to the exclusion of meeting your own.
- Excessive use of denial, especially of your own needs and feelings.
- Sacrificing your own identity for the sake of intimacy.
- Changing who you are to please others.
- Low self-worth.
- Being driven by compulsions.
- Substance abuse.
- Trying to control others with love or anger.
- Sacrificing your true self to keep the facade of your false self intact.
- Stress-related medical illnesses.

on the personality characteristics with which it is mixed. For example, a passive form of codependence leads to a person's taking on a martyr role. Suffering is accepted because it is in some way deserved. If you were a better person, then others would treat you better; if others treat you poorly, that is your punishment for your unseen flaws. An aggressive form of codependence could lead you to take on more of a persecutor role. Since you are still operating from the belief that other people's behavior is your responsibility, you try to make life so miserable for others that they are forced to change and start behaving the way you want them to.

There can be no single picture of codependent behavior, since the core dynamics of a distorted relationship to willpower and a sacrifice of your identity can take many forms. In clinical practice, we quickly learn that most personality problems have a thousand ways of masquerading as something else. This is part of what makes them a problem. Codependents are masters at masquerading and hiding their actual intentions and real selves, and they thus defy superficial descriptions. But no matter what form it takes, it is the codependence that makes you look capable and in control when inside you're feeling that you're in shambles. It is what leads you to please other people instead of loving them.

It's important for ACAs to take the causes of codependence seriously for three reasons. First, most of us learn what we see. The codependent characteristics of our parents gradually get crystallized into our own personalities, and we eventually come to see these characteristics as normal. Contact with the alcoholic family is no longer needed to keep your own codependence alive. A major commitment of time and energy is required to free yourself from its effects.

Second, codependence diminishes your capacity to deal effectively with the stress in your life. It turns normal problems into sources of great stress. As a CoA, not only did you experience far more stress than is normally encountered during childhood, but you were also taught ways of dealing with that stress that compound the effects it has on your life. By ignoring physical abuse from a parent, for example, you inadvertently became more likely to continue the pattern with your own children.

Third, as an ACA you almost certainly have elements of codependence affecting your life that have been carried over from the past to the present. A critical step in recovery is to take an honest look at the forces within you that are keeping your codependence alive.

SYMPTOMS OF CODEPENDENCE

The major signs of codependence are changing who you are to please others, feeling responsible for meeting others' needs at the expense of your own, low self-esteem, being driven by a variety of compulsions, and the same use of denial typically seen in active alcoholics.

Changing Who You Are to Please Others

Codependents exist through their relationships with other people. Being able to please someone else is their only avenue to feeling real. One depressed widow expressed this codependent perspective in a simple equation when she said, "I used to be half of something wonderful. Now I'm half of nothing, and half of nothing *is* nothing."

Many CoAs have watched a nondrinking parent slip into such profound codependence that they became as emotionally distant as the alcoholic parent. As a codependent, you are split between two worlds: the facade you show others, and the chaos or emptiness of your life underneath. The facade creates an appearance of being in control, competent, and worthwhile. It is constantly modified to give other people the impressions you think will please them. This facade can become so highly developed that you mistake the false version for your real self, while your real self remains hidden behind this facade and gradually withers away until only a sense of emptiness exists. When this happens, codependents always agree with whomever they're with, always want to do what pleases others, have no opinions themselves, and end up having no sense of self that is substantial enough for them to be in relationships with others.

An ACA with these symptoms told of having gone grocery shopping with a woman he wanted to impress. When they got to the freezer section, she asked if he liked ice cream. He said yes enthusiastically, but he didn't know what to do when she reached for a box of chocolate ice cream. He hated chocolate but was afraid to say so. Instead, he began arguing internally with his own feelings, telling himself that he had not tried any chocolate for several years and might like it now. He decided he would try it again rather than risk disappointing her.

Feeling Responsible for Meeting Other People's Needs at the Expense of Your Own

Codependents are so other-directed that they get more upset if someone else's needs go unmet than if their own do. This is not simple generosity, although many codependents excuse it as such. True generosity stems from loving your neighbors in the same way you love yourself. Codependents love their neighbors far more than they love themselves, and this can never be anything more than a superficial form of love—a form of love that is actually motivated by fear that the other person may leave you. If you are codependent, you become highly sensitive to other people's needs. This sensitivity may help you earn a living as a nurse or a teacher. If you do not work directly in one of the helping professions, you may still be the person everyone at your workplace can rely on, come to for help, and count on to accept extra work in a crunch. You probably enjoy being seen in this way, but you also suffer from not knowing how to say no when you should.

When it comes to your family, you're more aware of their need to have you home than of your own need to be with them. By constantly changing who you are in order to please them, you pay less and less attention to your own desires. You feel pulled on from every imaginable direction. You may wish that you had just ten minutes at the end of the day when you could do what *you* want to do. Unfortunately, when faced with ten minutes of free time, many ACAs become very uncomfortable. Unless they're taking care of other people's needs, they don't know what to do.

Low Self-Esteem

If parents are too preoccupied (with alcohol or with the alcoholic) to focus attention on their children as individuals, it becomes likely that the children will not be able to regard themselves as worthwhile later on in life. The widow who said that she is nothing now that she is no longer part of a couple demonstrates the abysmal lack of worth that codependents feel. If you are a codependent, you please other people because you believe that no one would choose to be with you unless you are serving them. You constantly feel you must earn their love, and you neglect your own needs because you do not feel that you are worthy enough to deserve to have your own needs met.

Codependents suffer low self-esteem for two reasons. First, they have turned their identities over to other people to such a degree that they often have very little sense of self to esteem. Second, codependents often enter into relationships with less than fully mature partners, people who because of their own inadequacy, shame, or self-centeredness require someone else to cater to them. After all, who else would choose to become partners with someone who borrows their identity from those around them and constantly tries to please in order to feel worthwhile? For the codependent, such partners are not good risks.

If you are going to place your sense of self-worth in the hands of someone else, it's an especially bad choice to team up with an active alcoholic. As long as the disease is active, it's impossible for a codependent to please an alcoholic enough to make him or her stop drinking. Whenever the drinking returns, codependents see this as further evidence of their own lack of worth. The equation in a codependent's mind is "If I loved my partner enough or the right way, he (or she) would not drink." All children of alcoholics have felt this way about their parents, and many of us had mothers or fathers who also felt this way about their spouses.

Driven by Compulsions

If you are a codependent, you feel little sense of choice in your life. You feel compelled to keep the family together when someone is blowing it apart by drinking. You feel compelled to keep the drinking hidden in order to save yourself and the family from shame. You may even feel compelled to drink!

Compulsive working, eating, risk taking, spending, gambling, sexuality, religiosity, housecleaning—the compulsions codependents feel are endless because the activities themselves are of only secondary importance. It does not matter whether the activity undertaken is work, exercise, or play; the underlying compulsion is the same.

Compulsions serve two purposes for codependents. First, they add drama to your life. If your sense of self is insubstantial, the drama of a compulsion temporarily gives you a feeling of being more fully alive. Simple activities such as eating nutritious food, working enough to gain satisfaction and adequate income, or shopping for new clothing are transformed into dramatic morality plays. The struggle that can be waged between yourself and the target of your compulsion can become very intense and can produce the vital, exciting rush of an adrenaline high.

Second, compulsions occupy a lot of time and effectively block us from becoming aware of deep, painful emotions. By feeling compelled to do everything possible to make the family look normal, codependents have no time left over to look deeper inside themselves to see how they really feel about what is happening to them. Many ACAs have grown up having both parents be out of touch with their real feelings. One parent was drinking compulsively, and the other was compulsively trying to maintain a good family facade. Both were unwilling to admit to themselves the depth of pain they were feeling.

Codependent Denial

Codependents tend to deal with problems largely through denial ("How could he be an alcoholic? He's never lost his job") and willpower ("If only I get this promotion and we can buy a bigger house, she'll be happy and cut down on her drinking"). The spouse of an alcoholic may keep close tabs on how much the partner is drinking and do something to divert attention whenever it looks like the partner is getting drunk. The alcoholic may initially like this added attention and may temporarily control the drinking. But then the alcoholic starts sneaking drinks. When the spouse notices this, he or she starts pouring bottles down the drain. The alcoholic is initially controlled by this but then finds new places to hide bottles. Completely focused on the alcoholic, the codependent begins feeling worse because the efforts to stop the alcoholic's drinking have not been creative enough to work. The codependent is denying the knowledge that the alcoholic is controlled by the disease, and the family desperately needs outside professional help. It is this denial that keeps the codependent trying to overpower the problem through force of will.

THE CORE DYNAMICS OF CODEPENDENCE

Codependence stems from two core dynamics that lie deep within one's personality: a distorted relationship to willpower, and the presumption that you must sacrifice your own identity to achieve intimacy with others.

Distorted Relationship to Willpower

To explore what is meant by a distorted relationship to will-power is to embark on the path toward recovery that every alcoholic and every child of an alcoholic must travel to find true freedom from the effects of the disease.

Paul and Irene illustrate the distorted relationship to willpower that is central to both active alcoholism and code-pendence. Paul was about to complete a twenty-eight-day hospital treatment program for his alcoholism, which had been out of control since he had started drinking at age sixteen. Asked what he would do when the impulse to drink returned, Paul proudly said, "I haven't wanted to drink since the day I got into treatment." Pressed about what he plans to do if he does have the urge to drink again, Paul looked indignant and said, "I just won't let that happen. I won't let myself want a drink." His wife, Irene, had the same attitude toward her anger at having been battered repeatedly for the last ten years. "I'm just going to bury the past. Being angry about it doesn't do any good. It doesn't change anything. Besides," she confided privately, "it could make Paul feel so guilty that he might go back to drinking."

Paul and Irene are convinced that their willpower can control all manner of things, especially their emotional lives, over which willpower simply has no direct control. It is help-ful to explore the role this distorted relationship to willpower plays in alcoholism in order to better understand the more general role it plays in codependence.

Alcoholism results from an interplay between two fac-tors. First, there are limits to the amount of alcohol each of us can drink without doing damage to ourselves. These limits differ widely from person to person. Those of us who develop or have inherited brain chemistries that do not tolerate alco-hol at all have the disease of alcoholism. Second, people have very different reactions to these limits. Some never recognize that there are any limits. Others recognize that these limits exist but refuse to accept them. The inability or unwillingness to recognize and accept limitations is not the cause of alcoholism, but it does represent the major barrier to recovery.

Active alcoholics almost universally interpret their inability to drink without losing control as a sign of inadequate willpower. Most everyone else in our society agrees with them. Considering that we live in an era that glamorizes the power of will, this is sad but understandable. Positive thinking and the human-potential movement often encourage us to believe that there are no limits to what we can accomplish through strength of will, from financial success, self-esteem, and spiritual enlightenment to curing cancer. However, this overwhelming devotion to willpower leaves little room for the Zen perspective, which freely recognizes the reality of limitations and teaches us not to waste energy resisting what cannot be changed. Without this perspective to balance our faith in willpower, we lose the humility that stems from being just human, not God.

Many nonalcoholics have difficulty understanding why alcoholics fail to see the damage they are doing by drinking more than they can tolerate. They think, "How could they be so stupid?" or "Why are they so weak?" Most alcoholics ask the same questions and often judge themselves harshly for having no good answers.

Alcoholics resist recognizing their limitations for several reasons. First, there is denial. Alcohol has invaded the alcoholic's psychological makeup, providing the primary avenue to a temporary sense of relaxation and feeling normal. The alcoholic can hang on to this comfort only by denying the problems that taking this avenue creates. Furthermore, the alcohol's effect on the brain makes it harder to break the denial.

In addition, the same stigma that surrounds alcoholism once surrounded tuberculosis and cancer—and today surrounds AIDS. Alcoholism is still seen as a result of psychological or moral defects and continues to be judged as a sign of weakness. What person would not resist recognizing his disease to avoid this stigma?

Because alcoholism sets one apart from others, the thought of being alcoholic is a tremendous blow to anyone's self-image. The same reaction can be seen among diabetics, some of whom react to their diagnosis by feeling defective and inferior. We do not like facing our limitations, especially if they appear arbitrarily imposed on us.

Finally, active alcoholics believe that the most important means of regaining their self-esteem is to prove they are not alcoholic. A tremendous battle ensues, in which being able to drink without losing control becomes the only true measure of self-worth. They drink beer instead of hard liquor. They change jobs or move to different parts of the country ("Everyone drinks in New York; I had to get out of there"). They only drink on weekends or only let themselves get falling-down drunk once a month. Only a small percentage of alcoholics give up all efforts to regain control; they either die quickly or are driven into treatment. *Once a person's self-esteem gets tied up in the ability to control drinking, the problem of alcoholism has taken root.*

In spite of their stereotypical out-of-control image, alcoholics are actually often obsessed with regaining control or denying that they have lost control. If there are ten ways to solve a problem, active alcoholics will focus on the way requiring the most willpower. For example, they often feel that using AA to get sober is less meaningful than if they stop drinking on their own. Their ideal is someone with so much willpower that he can continue drinking without losing control. Alcoholics are convinced that it is a matter of insufficient willpower that leads them to drink to excess, and their codependent spouses and friends thoroughly support this viewpoint. This belief that alcoholism can be controlled by willpower is as absurd as telling a diabetic to try harder to make insulin and control his blood sugar on his own. The very definition of a disease is that it cannot be eliminated by conscious choice.

To reject the notion that there are limits to what will-power can help you accomplish in any one part of your life is to become less able to deal effectively with the limits it has in the rest of your life. Paul and Irene are good examples. Each of them thinks that exerting control over the impulse to drink and trying to get rid of such feelings as Irene's anger are part of being normal. Alcoholics and codependents often confuse having control over their facades with being normal. In Paul and Irene's case, this belief has also led to trying to control how the other is behaving and feeling so that the relationship will look normal. Most people see willpower as the mental equivalent of muscles, and thus as something that can be strengthened through exercise. It's true that I can strengthen my back to lift more weight if I'm willing to discipline myself to a program of exercise. But I am able to do this only within certain limits. I'll never be able to lift the Empire State Building, for example. Muscles and willpower are both tools, and tools must be used properly if they are to be effective.

How do you know whether your failure to solve a problem is due to a lack of willpower or to an attempt to use willpower in an area where it has no application? It's normal to be confused about this distinction, since there are no hard-and-fast guidelines to follow. But no one is more confused about this than active alcoholics, codependents, and their children. While the distinction may be subtle, it is critical. Without an understanding of it, we're likely to waste a lot of energy banging our heads against brick walls while failing to take effective action when we should. The universe dictates limits to our willpower in dealing with the physical world, other people, and even aspects of ourselves.

It comes as a total surprise to many people that the process of recovery opens up to us only when we recognize that we are also powerless in many areas.

The Physical World

To begin with extremes, we are unable to affect the weather or to reverse gravity by our force of will. We are equally unable to lower mortgage-interest rates, raise the Dow-Jones average, or change the course of world events through sheer determination. We all know these things, but we usually don't spend time thinking about them; it's uncomfortable to be fully aware of how many of the forces pulling and pushing on us lie beyond our control.4

Other People

When we realize we have absolutely no direct control over the feelings another person has, the limitations of willpower become more clear. We cannot make another person be happy or angry. We might make ourselves behave kindly toward someone to please them. However, if the person is depressed or preoccupied, even our best efforts would be powerless to make them feel happy.

The inability to control other people's behavior is amply demonstrated every time you wish an infant would stop crying and go to sleep or when you try to force a child to study. It is also proven every time you try to use force of will to get an alcoholic to stop drinking. The reason we can't control how others act is because we have no control over their motivation. There is no more frustrating pursuit on earth than trying harder and harder to supply the motivation for another person to stop killing themselves with alcohol. Whether or not the change occurs rests on whether the other person has the motivation to make it occur.

Ourselves

There are limits to how much control you have over your physical body. Your height and sex are dictated to you, and although your weight is under some control, you certainly can't either gain or lose pounds by willpower alone. What willpower can do is determine much of your behavior. If the motivation is present, you can actively choose to change your weight by controlling what and how much you eat. In a similar way, when the impulse to drink arises, you have control over how you react to that impulse. Your willpower influences whether you walk into a bar or into an AA meeting.

The discomfort of facing how little power our will has to directly influence our lives increases when we begin to accept that willpower has virtually no ability to control our feelings and motivations. You cannot decide that you will wake up in ecstasy tomorrow morning or that you will begin to like chocolate ice cream if you have never liked it before. Just because you have read that forgiveness is necessary to heal your wounds, you cannot force yourself to stop being angry at your parents. You cannot force yourself to be motivated to enter recovery.

Your feelings and motivations are dictated to your conscious mind from deep within yourself, from regions of your mind that reach back into the past and beyond your ability to control what emerges. This is why the conscious mind has frequently been likened to a rider on the back of a wild horse. Over time, the two might begin to work in tandem. But until that time comes, the best the rider can do is to stay committed to holding on for the full course of the ride and to not abuse the horse for its refusal to submit.

What we *can* control by force of will is whether or not we pay attention to our feelings. A wife might become conscious of feeling angry at her husband for drinking every night. She is scared by this anger, fearing that it might lead to hard feelings on his part or to a fight and separation. To protect herself, she decides her anger is not justified, since he works all day and deserves to relax any way he wants once he gets home. She wills herself not to be angry anymore, but this is an illusion; she is simply willing her conscious mind to ignore the anger. That anger will remain in the unconscious until it is resolved or released in some manner.

Although these distinctions between what willpower can and cannot accomplish may appear elementary to some people, they are far from clear to CoAs. For CoAs and their parents, willpower is the royal road toward self-esteem and can be extended into every aspect of their lives, if only there is enough of it. To their way of thinking, willpower can determine how one feels about the world and how other people feel and act.

The prototypical interaction for this grandiose perspective on willpower occurs between CoAs and their alcoholic parents. Our parents sincerely believed that they drank because of outside circumstances—not enough money, a bad job, screaming kids, problems with a spouse. As a CoA, you grew up in a sea of misconceptions about what you can and cannot control.

Once you believe you are the cause of your parent's drinking, you will begin to experiment with what you think you can do to make your parent *stop* drinking. When your efforts fail, you'll attribute this to not having tried hard enough. You will redouble your determination and try to exert even more force of will to change things. In effect, you simply adopt—lock, stock, and barrel—the same coping strategy that is used unsuccessfully by the alcoholic. You become a codependent.

Sacrificing Identity for Intimacy

A useful way to approach the second core dynamic of codependence—sacrificing identity in the search for intimacy—is to look at its representation in classical mythology. The myth of Narcissus has been used as a symbol of self-centeredness since Sigmund Freud began writing about what he called "narcissism" in 1914. However, the original myth contained a second important figure, Echo, who has rarely received much attention. (Perhaps it is simply another manifestation of what Narcissus represents that led to the myth's being named after him alone!)

When Narcissus was born, his mother visited the oracle at Delphi and asked how long her son would live. "As long as he shall not come to know himself," the oracle answered. Under the shadow of this cryptic pronouncement, Narcissus grew into a beautiful youth, one whom all the maidens longed to have. But he would have none of them. He carelessly scorned those who were attracted to him, never responding to their love. Perhaps he instinctively knew that it is through the intimacy of loving others, and allowing them to love us, that we truly come to know ourselves.

Echo, the fairest of the wood nymphs, had a gift for entertaining others with her gay chatter. But she had gotten into difficulty one day with Zeus's wife, Hera, who suspected that Echo was chatting in order to keep her occupied while Zeus slipped out to the woods with several lovely nymphs. In a rage, Hera cursed Echo to speak only when she was repeating what others had already said. She would always have the last word, but she would never be able to speak the first. Echo became completely reactive, unable to initiate any interaction with others.

When Echo fell in love with Narcissus, she could not speak to him of her love. Instead, she followed him about silently, lovesick, wondering how she could attract his attention. At last her chance came when she heard him call out for his companions, "Is anybody here?" From behind a tree she repeated, "Here . . . here." He looked about and saw no one. "Whoever you are, come to me," he called. This was Echo's moment. She stepped out from behind the tree, motioned to Narcissus, and said, "Come to me."

Narcissus, who previously had never had to make the slightest effort to resist responding to a beautiful maiden's love, was touched by Echo. This made her particularly dangerous to him, and he turned away in anger, saying, "I will

die before I give you power over me." Echo responded, plead-
ingly, with the only thing she could say, "I give you power
over me." When he left, she felt embarrassment and shame
for humbling herself and having been rejected.

Nemesis, the god of righteous anger, punished Narcissus
for his callousness toward Echo. He caused Narcissus to catch
sight of his own reflection in a still pool and to fall in love
with what he saw. Since it was his own reflection, the image
could never be held, and so he found his fate to be the same
as Echo's. Lingering by the pool and yearning after a lover
who scorned him, Narcissus gradually weakened and died.
Echo stood nearby, and when Narcissus bid a final "Fare-
well" to his image, Echo was able to bid him good-bye as well.

Echo's own fate was equally sad. After losing Narcissus,
she was never able to be comforted and began wasting away.
Her flesh eventually became insubstantial, and her bones
turned to stone. All that was left was a voice, which can be
heard to this day in lonely caves and canyons.

The popular understanding of narcissism is of a condition in which people are excessively enamored of themselves,
for which Narcissus was punished by the gods. A closer
reading reveals this to be a misinterpretation. Narcissus's
falling in love with his own image was his plight, but it was
his unwillingness to respond to the love of others that was the
transgression for which Nemesis punished him.

What is important to ACAs is that Narcissus had no
trouble scorning the love of others until he encountered Echo.
She got to him in a way that no one ever had. Why else would
he have felt anger and disgust as he screamed that he would
never give her power over him? It is not even clear why he
believed that Echo wanted such power. These are not the
actions of a man who is unaffected by another. Echo's feelings
for Narcissus penetrated his barriers, and he found himself
responding to her love against his will.

The central flaw in narcissism, as the myth shows, is not so much an overblown self-love—too many narcissistic people suffer from low self-esteem for this to be the case—as it is a self-centeredness and a failure in the narcissist to feel a deep sense of human connectedness with other people unless he sees aspects of himself in the other person. A narcissist feels no vital connection to people who are completely autonomous and different. It is only when he sees that the other person walks and talks like him, wears the same fashions, shares the same values, or "echoes" him in some other way that the narcissist begins to feel connected. When others are not sufficiently like them, narcissists pressure people to act more like they do. Many interpret this as evidence that narcissists use themselves as the ultimate standard by which to judge everyone else. The truth lies more in the fact that narcissists do not feel a strong sense of connection to other people unless those people are willing to be like them.

What makes this relevant to ACAs is that self-centeredness is at the core of the problem for active alcoholics who whittle down their relationships until they are connected only to people who share their own attitudes and denial about drinking. This is not to say that all alcoholics were narcissistic before they began drinking and that this caused them to become alcoholic. The truth is that any person in the active stages of alcoholism becomes increasingly self-centered. As our brains lose their sharpness, we lose the ability to understand that other people have different perspectives on the world than we do. Alcoholics gradually feel connected only to people who resemble them. Thus, Echo's fate is widely shared by members of alcoholic families.

Living with an active alcoholic is only one avenue for becoming codependent. The world is filled with people who seek connection with others by becoming reflections of them. In an effort to break their own isolation, they sacrifice their identities. By taking on the characteristics of others, they achieve a sense of intimacy. Like Echo, their ultimate fate is to become less and less substantial. They never learn to be themselves because they are constantly identifying with a false sense borrowed from whatever relationship they are in at the moment. All they gain for the sacrifice of their identity is an illusory sense of intimacy.

6.

A Time for Honesty: The Second Betrayal

Many ACAs are making significant changes in their lives today. This is understandable once you accept that the damage done to CoAs is not restricted to the past. The tragedy of past events is that they usually lead to living in ways that keep the wounds festering. This chapter will help bridge your awareness from events of the past that can never be changed to events in the present that you do have the power to change. Ending your denial of the past addresses the original betrayal. Coming to terms with the second betrayal requires greater awareness of the *self*-neglect you continue into the present. Developing a more empathetic view of yourself will launch you fully on the road to recovery.

When children grow up in an environment where their emotions are not recognized and treated as real, they don't develop the capacity to validate their own feelings. They become adults who are never sure what they're feeling. Their emotional lives are not fully real. Children require external validation of their feelings if they are ever to develop self-validation.

The irony is that when ACAs fail to validate their own feelings as adults, they are guilty of precisely *the same neglect toward themselves that they received from their parents.* The way your parents treated your feelings when you were a child becomes the way you treat your own feelings as an adult.

Thus, ACAs are twice betrayed: the first betrayal stems from their parents' neglect of their emotions when they were children, and the second betrayal stems from the way they neglect their feelings themselves as adults. Thus, while the original betrayers may no longer be around, ACAs carry on their betrayal themselves.

The most fundamental damage done to children stems not from abuse but from neglect. The consequences of childhood's pain will never be as great as the betrayal of never having that pain validated by others. Children are resilient, but they do not exist in a vacuum. Their health absolutely requires that they have someone to bond with throughout their development—someone who will reaffirm that bond by noticing and accepting what is unique and different in the child. It is through such bonding that we come to know ourselves, especially on an emotional level.

We all begin to develop a sense of identity early on, before we are capable of seeing ourselves as separate from others. During this phase, we need to see our smiles and our tears reflected on other people's faces in order to know that our feelings are real. We trust the validity of our feelings more when others respond to them. This validation is most needed from our parents. Unless they have someone else to notice what they are feeling and to label it accurately, children are essentially unable to become aware of their own emotions.

Only after the reality of our feelings has been established can our identity be separated from those around us. This two-stage process of establishing the reality of one's feelings and then forming a separate identity is facilitated by parents who are healthy enough to react spontaneously and demonstrably to the feelings arising from within the child, and then to remain bonded to the child even as the child separates his or her own identity from those of the parents. Neither actively alcoholic nor actively codependent parents can fully perform either of these functions.

Imagine what life would be like if you were a child born to Narcissus. Narcissus would connect with you only while you were reflecting his image. There would be no room to develop your own personality. If differences emerged, the bond with him would be broken, and there would be no one to appreciate the separate and real self you were becoming. In alcoholic homes, whenever the autonomous feelings of children begin to emerge, the self-centered parents are unable to maintain a direct connection with their children. As a CoA, to have your own feelings and to develop as a unique individual is to lose any connection with your parents—a price too heavy to pay early in life.

When the nonalcoholic parent is actively codependent, he or she can accentuate the problems created by the alcoholic. Imagine having Narcissus as a father and Echo as a mother. Not only would you be pressured by Narcissus to be as much like him as possible, but you'd also see Echo sacrificing her own identity for the sake of a relationship with her husband. The only model of intimacy supplied by Echo is self-betrayal.

The parent-child relationship itself is swallowed whole and becomes part of the ACA's core personality. The legacy of how your parents treated you can be seen in how you relate to your own feelings as an adult. When parents have denied your pain and anger, you will tend to deal with feelings by ignoring them. You may pride yourself on never getting angry and being able to put up with any amount of inconvenience and pain. If your parents were scared and overwhelmed by your feelings, as an adult you live in fear that your emotions are ready to erupt with destructive force. If parents treated your feelings as signs of weakness, during adulthood you feel shame whenever emotions arise. If your parents were unable to feel any connection with you unless you felt the same things they did, you now feel a profound uneasiness with any feelings you think other people are not also having.

Children are not born with self-esteem. It must be

learned. The best time to learn self-esteem is during the moments when a sense of self is first emerging. When this occurs, a sense of worth is built right into the core of your identity. Such a basic sense of self-worth comes from being bonded to parents who love you as much as they love themselves. When their own self-esteem is low, and they love their children more than themselves, the children learn to love others more than themselves.

Despite your past experiences, you can take steps today to begin building greater self-esteem into your identity if you are willing to let others love you openly. Too often ACAs attempt to use willpower to feel good about themselves or try to exterminate negative thoughts about themselves. Sometimes they will use someone else's love for them as a substitute for self-love. The road to recovery requires that you allow others to know who you are and to continue loving you until you can love yourself. The difficult part of all this is to have enough faith to allow others to truly know you—in detail and in the moment. When others have esteem for who we really are, we can begin to feel self-acceptance.

This image of ACAs perpetrating upon themselves the same attitudes their parents had toward them as children can provide you with a powerful perspective, one that can be the source of both great pain and new hope. The pain comes from recognizing that you are guilty of the very behavior you reject in your parents. To acknowledge that you have become what you most feared becoming is deeply deflating. Suddenly, the only avenue toward a more healthy relationship with yourself requires advancing beyond the relationship your parents were capable of having with you when you were a child. Moving beyond your parents means having to wrestle successfully with some of the same fears and problems that plagued them. Once you realize the difficulty of such change, you will have begun to lay the groundwork for empathizing with your parents and the fate with which they found themselves floundering.

Empathizing with your parents, however, is not nearly as critical as beginning to develop empathy for yourself. The child you were is still waiting to be seen, to be listened to, and to have his or her feelings validated. When ACAs say they do not want to explore the painful feelings connected with having grown up in an alcoholic family, they are continuing to turn their backs on the children they were. They are still leaving those children isolated and lost, in need of someone to tell their feelings to—someone to notice that they are crying.

Many ACAs become aware of the first betrayal but not of the second. Those who get stuck at this point accept that their anger and sadness are appropriate responses to what happened to them, but they continue to feel trapped by their past. They do not move beyond anger and bitterness. They know why they have developed problems, but they still have no hope of resolving them, since what happened in the past cannot be changed.

Now that you have read to this point, you may understand that your current problems emanated from your experiences as a child rather than from some essential flaw within yourself. But you may also believe that you have far deeper problems than you ever suspected and that these problems can never be solved. Expressing your pent-up anger and sadness will be gratifying for a time, and it is a critical beginning. However, it can also be sustained for years without producing any real change in your life. At some point, more is needed.

Acknowledging the second betrayal, self-neglect, is the eye of the needle through which ACAs must pass if they hope to achieve significant recovery. When they come face-to-face with their self-betrayal, they begin to understand what is meant by the phrase "Pain is inevitable, but misery is optional." The past cannot be changed, and memories of it will always be tinged with pain. But if you continue to be a victim to that pain, you help to keep it alive.

Converting past pain into current misery is avoidable. You can begin to have empathy for yourself as a child by listening more closely than ever to the feelings that still need to be validated. As an adult child of an alcoholic, you can bond with the child within and stop betraying his or her need for intimacy. You can begin to do this by pulling down the wall of denial and looking in detail at what happened to you in the past. The next step is to make friends with the child you were by accepting that child without judgment. This is the meaning of recovery.

It's never too late for the child within to benefit from finally gaining a sympathetic ear. It is as though the child you were has waited patiently inside, never giving up hope that someday someone would be there for it. Once you develop a willingness to listen compassionately to your own story, an entirely new relationship with yourself becomes possible. The feeling side of your personality is finally granted the right to be present. As your compassion grows for yourself as a child, the possibility of feeling compassion for all the softer, more spontaneous, and emotional aspects of yourself as an adult also increases. Today, ACAs are discovering through self-help groups and therapy how they can treat each other in a healing way by taking the risk of speaking openly about their experiences, their strengths, and their hopes.

Although it's important for you to come to terms with being the child of an alcoholic, it's equally important that you maintain an awareness that you are the *adult* child of an alcoholic. You can thus become the protector and the patron of the child within, treating that child with gentleness and caring. This action has great healing power, and ACAs often benefit tremendously from learning to parent themselves more effectively. I have seen recovering ACAs develop closer relationships with the children they were by taking themselves to the zoo, going to a kids' movie, or treating themselves to an ice-cream cone, just because those are the things no one ever did for them when they were children. In offering these gifts to themselves as children, they found that a trust developed between the adult and the child parts of themselves. Childlike qualities began to emerge more freely, since the child finally knew that there was a competent adult in the vicinity if anything got out of control.

GRIEF AND TRAUMA

A largely unrecognized reason why many ACAs remain cut off from their childhoods and the childlike nature alive within them is the special chemistry that results from the mixture of grief and trauma. It is important to understand how these two feelings reverberate with each other to close off the avenue toward recovery for many.

Grief refers to the feelings that occur in response to a significant loss. Not all grief is traumatic. Children who lose a parent to chronic illness may be in an environment that supports whatever feelings are present. Children in such an atmosphere still experience the intense feelings of loss, but they are generally spared an excessive sense of danger and anxiety about their own continued existence. A safety net, like that beneath a tightrope walker, is present throughout their experience. The rope still has to be walked and the grief still has to be felt, but there never has to be concern for one's own personal safety.

However, when the physical or emotional loss of a parent occurs in the unsafe atmosphere of an alcoholic home, children's fears are activated. The threat that a parent might lose control leads children to a state of anxious anticipation that even greater damage may occur. The constant pumping out of adrenaline to meet the challenge posed by the anticipated damage disrupts the natural grieving process, and the result is traumatic grief.

For many ACAs traumatic grief stands in the way of their being able to get back in contact with the childhood they abandoned so long ago. In the same way that a rock climber suddenly overcome by a phobic fear of height is paralyzed, a person suffering from traumatic grief is also paralyzed. Just as the climber needs to focus on only the next small step, the grief-stricken ACA must mourn bit by bit, not all at once. This is made impossible, however, when a single memory brings a flood of traumatic memories with it, creating intolerable levels of anxiety. The small steps needed to get down from the precipice produce too much anxiety to even be attempted. The process of mourning is thus blocked by the traumatic reactions, and grief remains unabated.

The following story illustrates how the second form of betrayal—the betrayal of self—can be stopped, even in the face of traumatic grief. This story will help you begin to look at what you, as an ACA, can do to begin promoting your own healing today.

Alice: The Beginning of Recovery

When she was five years old, Alice suffered a broken leg and required a full leg cast. The morning after the cast was put on, Alice complained to her parents that her leg hurt. But her father was suffering from a mammoth hangover, and her mother was torn between who needed the most care. She gave Alice a couple of aspirin with codeine and focused on keeping her husband from getting too irritable.

Since it was Saturday, Alice's father began drinking again shortly after he got out of bed. By afternoon he was roaring drunk, and a terrible fight broke out between Alice's parents as they began blaming each other for her accident. She went as long as she could without complaining about the pain again in order not to contribute to the arguing between her parents.

That night Alice woke up because of the pain and

lay in her bed whimpering. Her father had passed out
early in the evening and had awakened again in the
middle of the night. He was rampaging through the
house, kicking the wall and throwing chairs around.
Alice's mother crawled into bed with her and held her
tightly, trying to comfort her while at the same time
trying to comfort herself through Alice's innocent presence. When Alice's father finally quieted down and fell
asleep, her mother decided that it was far too late to take
Alice to the hospital or to bother the doctor with a phone
call. She gave the little girl a glass of wine to help her
get to sleep and then went off to bed herself.

The next day was a repeat of Saturday. Alice
remembers pleading with her father to take her to the
hospital, but he insisted that because she had broken her
leg she should expect to have a little pain. That night
Alice hardly slept at all. To this day she can describe in
great detail all the sounds she heard in the house that
night as she lay there alone, feeling her whole leg throb-
bing with each heartbeat. By morning she had finally
fallen asleep; when she woke up, her leg was less painful. Over the next two days she lost all feeling in her leg,
which naturally relieved the pain completely. What had
actually happened was that the cast had been put on too
tightly, so Alice's broken leg had swollen. Now the blood
supply to her leg had been cut off enough that the nerves
were beginning to die.

Several weeks later, the family was horrified to
discover a trickle of dark liquid oozing out of the toe of
Alice's cast. A foul odor had begun to come from her leg.
Her parents rushed her to the hospital; she remembers
being held down by her father so she could not watch
as the doctor removed her cast. The smell was overpow-
ering as the cast split apart; chunks of blackened muscle
were sticking to the cast and peeling off her leg. A nurse
passed out at the sight.

Alice remembered her father turning to the doctor and commenting on how difficult this must be for him. As an adult, she came to see her father's concern for the doctor's feelings rather than hers as the clearest example of how his life had been completely reduced to the impressions others had of him. He had come to be more interested in the facade surrounding himself and his family than with the realities behind that facade. Unfortunately, Alice was one of those realities. Advanced gangrene had developed in her leg, and amputation was eventually required. The stage was set for her to experience traumatic grief.

It is little wonder that Alice was into her mid-adult years before she could begin to resolve her feelings about her father's alcoholism. By that time, her personality was dominated by the beliefs that she could accomplish anything through grim determination and that whatever she accomplished would have to be done entirely on her own. This attitude served her well in her career, since she never allowed any barriers to stand in her way. But this style allowed little room for fun, never allowed anything to be accomplished easily, and left her unable to ask other people for help when she needed it. Unless things were achieved with a struggle, they didn't feel worthwhile. Over the years this mode of behavior began to wear Alice down and to alienate the people who cared about her.

When Alice first became aware of ACA issues, she was attracted to how well they described her internal life. She attended an Al-Anon meeting for ACAs and found herself alternating between being horribly bored and being shaken by intense anxiety, which she felt vibrating through the middle of her body. It was impossible for her to speak in the meetings without feeling that she would explode. After beginning to work with an individual therapist familiar with ACA issues, Alice was able to look for the first time at what it had been like to grow up in her alcoholic family. Whenever any feelings of sadness or anger began to stir in her, the intense anxiety superimposed itself and took over. The traumatic nature of Alice's grief continually interrupted the process of mourning. The only meaning she could derive from her childhood experience was that she was alone, in danger, and had to rely on her own determination in order to survive.

Alice was blocked from having any deep empathy for herself as a child. She was no more able to face the stark terror and loneliness she had felt during the events surrounding the amputation than her parents had been to face their own issues. Whenever she did try to listen to that small child's feelings, her anxiety level shot through the roof. Fortunately for her chances of recovery, Alice's grim determination became a valuable tool at this point. She had become determined to reclaim her feelings. At a workshop for ACAs, where she was able to tell her story openly, I offered Alice an opportunity to use psychodrama to re-create the family she lived in at age five. Despite a deep sense of apprehension, she chose to enter into the experience.

Alice's family tree was outlined on the blackboard. Other workshop participants were chosen to represent her parents, her brother and sister, and herself. Gradually, a concrete living sculpture of her family emerged as each person was taught the prominent characteristics of the family member he or she had been chosen to represent.

These "family members" were physically placed in positions that symbolized their relationships to one another. Alice's father hid behind the newspaper, except when he was drinking. When intoxicated, he swelled up until he was bigger than life, threatening everyone except Alice's sister, who in his eyes could do no wrong. The mother took a weak and submissive posture, requiring protection and comfort from her children whenever her husband became drunk. Her brother was filled with anxiety, and he dealt with this by constantly trying to please his father. Alice placed the woman she had chosen to portray herself off in a corner, lying almost in a fetal position, paralyzed by fear and generally ignored by everyone except her sister, who occasionally knelt down to check on how she was doing.

I guided Alice into the "sculpture," and walked her around each of the members of her family. As we did so, I asked her to report whatever feelings began to emerge. By allowing the reality of her earlier family situation to be this vivid again, Alice started to feel deep empathy for how neglected she looked as a five-year-old curled up in a fetal position. She began to tell her father how angry she felt, something she had never done in real life. To deepen her feelings further, Alice was asked to take her own place in the family sculpture by lying down in the corner. After she had assumed this position, a shudder racked her body. The emotions that had become unlocked were too intense for her to continue with, especially on top of what she was already feeling. She began to shut down and became more intellectual about what was happening. This was a protective mechanism that needed to be honored. Learning to protect herself in exactly this way as a child had prevented her from being even more overwhelmed by her fears.

After the family sculpture was disassembled and everyone returned to the present, other workshop participants spoke of being impressed by Alice's courage in facing such strong feelings and memories. It had never occurred to Alice that she was being courageous. She had already decided that she was a failure for having to shut off the feelings again. As she listened, others told her of their rage at watching her family be so absorbed by her father's alcoholism that no time or emotional energy was left over for a terrified five-year-old. Some wept as they told of how Alice's family reminded them of the pain and loneliness of their own childhoods.

What was happening to Alice as she listened to these reactions was hidden from everyone's view at the time, but it later proved to be profoundly significant. She was finally getting the validation for her childhood feelings that she had never previously experienced. By revisiting the realities of her childhood in the company of people who could be present for her, she had been able to get the external validation that had always been missing. Several weeks later, Alice had a striking dream in which she began seeing the rotting flesh of her leg as an expression of her father's illness and no longer as evidence that there was something wrong with who she was. She no longer judged herself for the fate that had befallen her, and she could now have empathy for the little girl she had been. Her recovery had taken an important step forward.

During Alice's childhood she had been hostage to her father's alcoholism, and his disease had led him to betray the trust she needed to place in him. He had only been able to relate to her as an extension of himself, and when her pain or her gangrenous leg violated the facade of normalcy that he felt obligated to show to the outside world, he paid little or no attention to her feelings. Alice eventually adopted the way her father treated her as the way she treated herself, and so she, too, began to betray herself. In essence, she began to treat her emotional life as though it were a child whom she should ignore in order to avoid embarrassment. As a result, her childhood remained hostage throughout much of her adult life as well. Alice was blocked from truly knowing herself and from finding any real peace. The second form of betrayal was continuing to turn the pain of earlier betrayal into chronic misery.

To deal effectively with her ACA issues, Alice needed to unlock her feelings and spontaneity. Since she was unable to validate this side of herself on her own, she needed to rely at first on external validation. Codependents rely too much on external validation (as already noted, they surrender their identities to others in relationships). So Alice was faced with the need to find a very special environment, one that she could be sure contained people who would accept whatever feelings she brought up. Once Alice had found such a group, she also needed to return temporarily to the time and events in her life when she began cooperating with holding her childhood self hostage. Finally, Alice needed to give this child back her voice. She needed to stop breaking trust with herself so that she could begin to change her life in a meaningful way.

Other people can play a vital role in this work by forming a validating link between ourselves and our feelings. The ultimate test is whether the ACA can eventually use this validation from others to help reestablish contact with the child he or she once was and then to embrace that child. We must give ourselves freedom, not to be whatever we think we should be but to be exactly what we are. Initially, this may mean feeling scared, lonely, sad, or angry. "To everything there is a season." By listening to these feelings without judging them, we can free the child within from being held hostage.

While this may seem like too much to hope for, too many people have experienced this freedom for the likelihood of recovery to be ignored. We have learned much from these people about the road to recovery. The first six chapters in this book have been designed to bring you to a general understanding of what the ACA must recover from. This understanding now sets the stage for you to look at the recovery process itself.

Part 3

The
Journey

We began with the promise of recovery, and the hope it brought enabled us to look back over the long, hard road we took through childhood. As past memories and feelings became real again, the possibility of healing began awakening. While you may not have felt this yet, the time is close.

The initial work of recovery involves preparing the soil. By exploring the effects of denial, stress, and codependence on your life, you have been laying the groundwork for a wonderful garden. Now that the process of healing is ready to grow within you, conscious attitudes of discipline and patience need to become the focus of your recovery. Once the garden has started to grow, there is much less that you can actively do. You can nurture the new growth, but you must allow it to proceed at its own natural pace. Nor can you choose the final form it will take. The outcome will be best if you can learn to enjoy the journey itself rather than focusing on what you think the goal should be.

Your healing takes place through the mind's natural healing processes. Chapter 7 outlines the factors that promote healing and then traces the predictable stages through which it passes. Much of the natural wisdom of recovering minds and hearts has been distilled in what are known as Twelve-Step self-help programs, which are the focus of chapter 8. The conscious effort to practice this wisdom in your daily life constitutes the discipline of recovery.

Aids to recovery are also available, and chapter 9 describes how professional treatment may benefit your life. While psychotherapy is unable to do the healing for you, it can provide you with unique experiences that call forth your own dormant powers. A good therapeutic relationship can be a crucible of recovery. The better you understand such a crucible, the more effectively you can make it work for you.

Finally, the lack of exposure that ACAs have had to healthy adult behavior leaves many people without a clear vision of recovery. People have asked me in all seriousness, "How would I know recovery if I saw it?" The Afterword points toward a vision of recovery by revisiting Huckleberry Finn. What would Huck's life as an adult have been like if he had followed the path of recovery far enough to find the freedom and balance that come from having healthy relationships with oneself and with the world?

7.

~~~~~~~~~~~~~~~~~~~~~~~~~~~~~~~~~~~

A Time to Trust:
The Road to Recovery

In Huckleberry Finn's world, there was no understanding of the special problems of ACAs. And until recently, most ACAs experienced no more understanding of their needs and conditions than Huck did. Today, however, there are more reasons than ever to feel hopeful. The road to recovery has been paved and widened into two lanes. One lane consists of self-help organizations, such as the powerful Twelve-Step programs for ACAs, patterned after Alcoholics Anonymous, and the other lane is the emerging field of therapy for ACAs. While it is up to each individual ACA to travel this road, there is a great deal of help available along the way.

Unlike Huckleberry Finn, ACAs today have easy access to other ACAs and to professionals who can support and guide them along the road to personal recovery.

Virginia is a member of this community of recovering ACAs. Her time to heal began when she entered a therapy group for ACAs. Her marriage was nearly over, largely because her husband wanted to have a family and she was too scared to consider taking this step. Virginia swore that she never wanted to pass on to a child what she had gotten from her parents: a lack of self-confidence and a bitterness that permeated her whole life. She had also been physically abused and didn't know if she could trust herself not to abuse

her own child. Virginia felt that the only way she could
protect her children was simply not to have any.

Today, Virginia has a beautiful two-year-old daughter
and looks forward to becoming pregnant again. She recounts
her journey and the positive path she is now on:

> I finally saw how much I was suffering from the bitter-
> ness I held toward my parents, and it no longer seemed
> like it was worth the price. You know, I don't think I
> have forgiven them. I just discovered that they started
> slipping off center stage as my own recovery grew. And
> when they were taken out of the center of my life, there
> was room for *me* for the first time. I realized how okay
> I am—okay enough to let my husband and my child into
> my life without worrying that I will contaminate them
> somehow. There are still a lot of things I do not like
> about myself, but I don't let them get in the way of
> having the things I really want to have in my life.

That's the promise of recovery.

Rod is another member of the ACA community. He
began his time to heal when he entered a Twelve-Step recovery program for compulsive eaters. Although Rod had never
been overweight, he nevertheless used food to avoid emotions. When he began to face his real feelings directly, he
realized how angry he was at his alcoholic parents. During the
first several years of his healing, he experienced excruciating
pain whenever he had to deal with his family, either in reality
or in his thoughts. Today, Rod has remarkably good relationships with some members of his family. His younger brother
moved across the country to work in his business. His mother
visits him on her own initiative, and the two have found that
they can talk together comfortably when Rod's father is not
present.

Although Rod's father seems to be going off the deep
end again with prescription-pill abuse, Rod has been able to

tell him exactly how it feels to have to watch him put his life in such danger. In one brief moment, his father looked out through a crack in the thick wall of denial he hides behind, and their eyes made direct contact. Rod's father confessed that he was afraid, too. Then the crack closed again. "I can't tell you how much that has meant to my life," Rod says. "Even though my father is probably going to kill himself soon, there was a moment when we met—and he told me that deep inside, he knows I am not the one who is crazy. I can let go of him now without feeling guilty." This is the promise of recovery.

Margaret is also a member of this community. Her time to heal began when a colleague asked her whether she was feeling fulfilled by her successful career as a divorce lawyer. Margaret was extremely good at helping couples reconcile their marriages (or at least to cooperate in a settlement and thus avoid a court battle). Her childhood years of feeling responsible for keeping her parents' marriage together had trained her well. Margaret's distaste for this work had grown to the point that she could barely get out of bed to make it to her office before noon.

Today, Margaret is preparing to take her vows as an Episcopal priest. Her law practice is barely a memory. "I now have a calling rather than a career, and I can devote myself to it without feeling drained. My life feels entirely different today. Perhaps I can best explain the difference by saying that if I found out I was going to die in six months, I would not change one detail of how I am living my life. I would still be here talking to you now, and I would look forward to the rest of my days just as much as I already am." That's the promise of recovery.

Another member is Ellen. When she read a book about CoAs and then entered individual therapy, her time to heal began. In her mid-thirties, Ellen seemed destined to a lifetime of short-term relationships with men who were unavailable to her, just as her alcoholic father remains emotionally unavailable to her despite twenty years of abstaining from drinking. Ellen's pattern of falling in love with married men and confirmed bachelors was so compulsive that she wanted therapy to help her learn how to live alone instead.

Today Ellen has just returned from her honeymoon. Soon after she started therapy, she realized how deeply she wanted an intimate relationship in her life and how much she feared it. By learning to protect herself from being overwhelmed by her father's continued intrusions into her life, Ellen gained enough confidence to begin a relationship with a man who was really available to her. "I never thought I was capable of being loved or that I deserved it. I don't know how my marriage is going to work out. I honestly believe that it will last. But whatever happens, I no longer have any doubts that I deserve to be loved as much as anyone else does." This, too, is the promise of recovery.

What all of these recovering ACAs have in common is an acceptance that they may never heal all of their wounds from childhood and a deep realization that ultimately this does not matter. Our healing depends as much on how we respond to those wounds as it does on the wounds themselves. Scars do not have to be eradicated in order for us to find freedom from them. ACA characteristics may still remain as initial reflexes to life's events, but we can learn to use these reflexes as a signal that something in our current life is activating the past. Then we can choose to react differently. The style of solving problems that develops as healing deepens is a way of finding peace with our limitations. Once this peace has been found, a whole new set of strategies for coping with life's difficulties becomes available.

The members of the community of recovering ACAs who have been described above are not projecting a facade; the peace they have found radiates from within. They affect people around them simply by allowing this peace to emerge from their hearts. As your own time to heal arrives, you will feel yourself respond more and more to the presence of this peace.

You will eventually come to know that this peace alone is powerful enough to set you free and restore your balance.

Reading this book may be an important part of your recovery, but the insights you gain into your life here are not sufficient for you to make the deep and lasting changes you are seeking. The unconscious habits you developed during childhood require that you make a disciplined commitment to change. Such a commitment takes time and necessarily involves becoming increasingly vulnerable to others who also value recovery. If you are to travel the road to recovery and truly know healing, you must abandon the idea of traveling alone.

STAGES OF RECOVERY

As recovery progresses, you will pass through five major stages.* First is the survivor stage, in which you are still firmly stuck in denial and much of life seems to be a struggle, whether you are winning or losing. Next is the reidentification stage, which begins with acceptance of the label of "adult child of an alcoholic" and ends with the acceptance of the need for a thorough reexploration of the proper role that willpower should play in your life. The core-issues stage is third. Here, the reexploration begun in the previous stage spreads to all aspects of your life, until you realize that your efforts to control the universe are actually the cause of many of your current problems. In the integration stage, the beliefs that attack your self-esteem are replaced by beliefs that support it, and your own sense of integrity, not what others may think of you, becomes your guide. Finally, in the genesis

*I wish to express a special indebtedness for Stephanie Brown's description of the stages of recovery from alcoholism, and for the work of Herbert Gravitz and Julie Bowden on recovery stages for ACAs, both of which have contributed to the material in this chapter.

stage, spiritual concerns come to the fore and begin to take on new importance. Each of these five stages is discussed in depth in the pages that follow.

Survivor Stage

If you are still unrealistically resisting the fact that your parent is an alcoholic and you're refusing to look at how you feel about his or her drinking, you are probably in the survivor stage. To appear normal and avoid being overwhelmed by anger and sadness, you keep your feelings and spontaneity tightly reined in. Denial seems necessary for sheer survival.

Because denial blinds you to the actual source of your pain, the survivor stage is characterized by a sourceless sense of discomfort. ACAs in this stage often search restlessly for something to lessen their pain, something to give them a feeling of belonging, something to fill the void inside. You may become a self-improvement or workshop junkie, constantly trying the latest fad method for becoming more assertive or for building self-esteem. In an effort to deaden your unease with yourself and the world, you may turn to compulsive behaviors (such as eating, shopping, gambling, or sexuality), compulsive rationality, or compulsive use of alcohol or drugs. At this point, healing becomes simultaneously more critical and more difficult to achieve.

The central problem in the survivor stage is identity: in this stage, you are basing your identity on what you are *not*. You identify yourself as not an ACA, or as nothing like your alcoholic parent. Negative identities are never a source of real comfort; they never lead to feeling normal about oneself. The task facing you in the survivor stage is to accurately label who and what you are so that you can begin to discern the real sources of pain in your life. Rigid honesty is required. As long as denial obscures your view of reality, you are left without a chance of healing yourself.

Reidentification Stage

If you have begun to identify yourself as an ACA, either as a result of reading this book or of having learned about adult children of alcoholics in some other way, you are entering the reidentification stage. I use the term *reidentification* to emphasize that healing begins with a shift in who you see yourself to be. There is a subtle but critical distinction between acknowledging that you have an alcoholic parent and acknowledging that you are the child of an alcoholic. In the former you place the attention outside yourself, concentrating on your parents' betrayal of your childhood; in the latter you focus your attention inward on your own self-betrayal. While it is important to understand the first betrayal, it is the second that keeps the legacy of the past alive, disrupting your life today. Ultimately, you must focus on your deepest self if your time to heal is ever to arrive.

A comparison between ACAs and alcoholics is helpful here, since recovery for each passes through identical stages. Many alcoholics penetrate their denial, take on the label of being alcoholic, and stop drinking. But unless they also acknowledge the tremendous issues they have with control, their healing stops. They remain dry, which is an uncomfortable state of always having to maintain control. Much of their alcoholic behavior remains, even though they are no longer drinking. This means that they remain irritable, arbitrary, controlling, intrusive, and in denial. Their recovery has stalled after the first portion of the reidentification stage.

A similar state exists for ACAs. Many ACAs acknowledge that their parent is alcoholic, but find that, years later, they are still stuck in their feelings of rage, loss, and abandonment. The healing process has derailed for them. By failing to make the subtle but critical shift to seeing yourself as the *child* of an alcoholic, you miss recognizing that everything you know about control and willpower needs to be called into question. The second portion of the reidentification stage requires an acknowledgment that your relationship to will-power was learned at the knee of someone who knew nothing about such matters. When you face the enemy, like Pogo, you discover that it is you after all.

The second aspect of the reidentification stage is truly the eye of the needle. You are faced with a task that is so subtle it is almost ineffable, yet it is absolutely crucial to the full healing of your spirit. If you think I am overstating the importance and difficulty of this second task, I can only re-spond by saying that I have chosen my words here with extreme care. I believe that no less than your emotional, spiritual, and even physical health rests on how you respond to the issues of control that face you at this point.

The eye of the needle is a matter of "willingness" versus "willfulness." ACAs who are stuck in rage, loss, and aban-donment are somehow still resisting these feelings, whether they are aware of this resistance or not. They are not yet *willing* to have their rage, their loss, or their abandonment. They secretly hope that, by having these feelings, they may somehow gain control over them, or reverse the past, or get their parents to recant and feel sorry. I have known many ACAs who willfully push themselves through their feelings as quickly as possible, trying to "make" themselves heal accord-ing to their own time frame. It does not work to have your feelings in order to heal. You must be willing to have your feelings simply because they are real. If you have them for any other reason, you are still using them to manipulate your world. You have only refined your efforts to control what is real. Greater sophistication in the control game only gets you more years of misery.

It is unlikely that anyone who refuses to explore self-help meetings for ACAs or to enter into therapy will success-fully progress through the final steps of the reidentification stage and on to later stages of recovery. It would, of course, be foolish to suggest that these are the only two lanes on the road to recovery. The miracle of healing has an infinite number of paths along which it can occur. Placing emphasis on the word *refuses* can help make the statement beginning this paragraph more understandable. If your life is not working as well as you would like it to but you refuse to take advantage of the most understood and successful forms of help available, then this is almost certainly further evidence that part of your problem is caused by your overwhelming need to be in control of your own recovery. However, such control is a paradox, since recovery entails voluntarily giving up the vain attempts at overcontrol that are currently causing problems in your life.

If the paradoxes of willpower and control confronted during the latter portion of the reidentification stage seem confusing, do not be dismayed. Many people have been thwarted by trying to understand these concepts intellectually. Real paradox exists, and it cannot be resolved by any exercise of reason. Rather, it must be lived with to be fully comprehended.

Core-Issues Stage

During the survivor and reidentification stages, your initial recovery consisted of ending the denial of your parent's alcoholism and its effects on you and accepting that a new perception of willpower is possible. Taking this leap of faith and accepting realistic limits to what you can control is crucial to promoting your recovery. The core-issues stage begins when you accept that further healing is a constant process. If your first leap of faith ends up being the last one you take, you get stuck. Healing only proceeds when you are willing to continue taking leaps into the unknown.

If all of this feels a bit overwhelming, I remind you of the stunned feeling of alcoholics who think that becoming abstinent is the greatest achievement possible. However, in becoming abstinent they have only begun their journey, in which they must face the many problems caused by their alcoholism and their misperceptions of willpower.

Another way of looking at the core-issues stage is to see it as the time when both ACAs and alcoholics begin to deal with the full extent of their codependence. Healing proceeds from this point through an exploration of all the ways in which a distorted relationship to willpower have influenced your life. It means discovering how self-will has choked the life out of you and your relationships. Having difficulty in trusting others and in being spontaneous, maintaining a protective facade, denying your emotional and physical needs, basing your self-esteem on how others see you, and feeling overly responsible for others—all of these are control issues for codependents.

The core-issues stage goes beyond changes in attitude and becomes a time for action. It calls upon you to experiment with being spontaneous, to allow yourself to have needs, and to stop acting out of a sense of guilt and responsibility for others. Each time you face a new jump into the unknown, all the fears you felt during the reidentification stage will return. When this happens, remember how you took a leap that first time despite your fears. The core-issues stage is a time to practice entering the unknown as often as possible, until it has become second nature to you. It will then have become a new way of life.

Your old way of handling this instruction would have been to force yourself to be spontaneous and to ignore how embarrassed or scared it made you feel. Such a reaction constitutes the same mistaken attempt at control that you are trying to relinquish. The new way of approaching things is to pay enough attention to how bad it feels not to be spontaneous that you eventually become willing to try something new. Similarly, your old way of doing things would call for you to force yourself to stop pleasing people by ignoring how scared you feel when you can no longer use their impressions of you as a guide for action. The new way calls for you to stop pleasing others in order to see what it feels like to let them form their own impressions of you, without effort on your part.

The core-issues stage is often a long and laborious reexploration of what legitimately lies under human control and what does not. As healing progresses during this stage, the number of areas in which you are effective in your life increase. You will be wasting less and less energy in trying to change things beyond your control. Your emotional life will awaken and will begin to ebb and flow with a life of its own.

Much of the work at the core-issues stage focuses on how you can enter relationships from the perspective of your real self rather than hiding behind the facade of your false self. Attempting to make intimate relationships work by trying to control what others feel or what impressions they have of you is a central theme in codependence. Completion of the core-issues stage depends on a willingness to enter into intimate relationships noncodependently. Relationships with others in the recovering community are useful places to experiment with new ways of being vulnerable. The goal of this stage of recovery is to forever abandon the codependent belief that you can do intimate relationships by yourself.

Integration Stage

As you progressed through the core-issues stage, one cherished belief after another was challenged and dropped. You may have begun to feel like a ship that has lost its moorings. Where are the beliefs that will replace those that have been found ineffective and discarded? During the stage of integration, new beliefs are developed and woven into the fabric of a new approach to life.

Up to this point, your fundamental beliefs have systematically attacked your sense of self-esteem. Every ACA is familiar with the "committee" inside his or her head, composed of all the voices that put out a constant stream of negative beliefs. Whenever you accomplish something, your committee reminds you that it wasn't really that difficult, or that you could have done it sooner or better. Whenever people pay you a compliment, your committee reminds you that you have only pulled the wool over those people's eyes or that they don't have very high standards. Every time you feel good about yourself, your committee quickly reminds you of things you are not doing well, just to keep you from getting a swelled head. The committee clicks into action at the smallest sign of self-esteem.

During the integration stage, a new voice develops, one that legitimizes self-acceptance instead of attacking it. This new voice comes from two sources: the transformation of liabilities into assets, and the emergence of a sense of integrity as the guiding principle for behavior. Both of these come to you as gifts. They cannot be forced to appear before their time. They simply begin to appear as the work of the core-issues stage comes to an end.

The first of these, the transformation of liabilities into assets, provides an unexpected answer to the commonly asked question "How do I get rid of ACA characteristics?" The answer is that you don't *have* to get rid of them. Trying to *get rid* of these characteristics is the old way of dealing with these issues, the one based on your belief that you could make your life go better if you had direct control over who and what you are. Once you've accepted that many of your ACA characteristics were essential in order for you to have survived the stresses of childhood, why would you want to jettison them? The healing during the first three stages has freed you from being a prisoner to these survival skills, and you now have the ability to use them or not, depending on your current needs. For example, extreme sensitivity to others' feelings can be used to great advantage by ACAs in the helping professions once these ACAs are no longer locked into feeling responsible for everyone else. Hypervigilance can be a useful tool in searching for people who have enough healing in their own lives that you can trust them in relationships. The tendency to control everything can be relied on to keep important aspects of your life organized. Many of your ACA characteristics, if they are allowed to play a proper role in your life, can become assets. Their ability to sustain you need never be relinquished, especially once they are no longer smothering you.

Previously, your behavior has been guided largely by how you think other people will react to you. In the process of dismantling your wall of denial, a new experience enters your life—a feeling of greater integrity. As you acknowledge more of the realities in your past and present life, this sense of integrity grows. You become conscious of the feeling of greater peace that comes with becoming your true self. You accept your feelings, rather than fleeing into the psychic numbing that makes your life more distant and less real.

The integration stage involves switching over to an internal standard for choosing how to be in the world. You choose to reveal your feelings or not, depending on how each choice makes you feel about yourself. The system of beliefs that supports your right to live by an internal standard takes many forms, and the work to be done in the integration stage is to fashion your own personal bill of rights. The following items are frequently included:*

Personal Bill of Rights

1. Life should have choices beyond mere survival.
2. I have a right to say no to anything when I do not feel ready or when it's unsafe.
3. Life should not be motivated by fear.

---

*Items on this list derive from the work of Claudia Black, Herbert Gravitz, Julie Bowden, and Jael Greenleaf, as well as from the author's own experience.

4. I have a right to all of my feelings.
5. I am probably not guilty.
6. I have a right to make mistakes.
7. There is no need to smile when I cry.
8. I have a right to terminate conversations with people who make me feel diminished and humiliated.
9. I can be healthier than those around me.
10. It's okay for me to be relaxed, playful, and frivolous.
11. I have a right to change and grow.
12. It is important to set limits and to take care of myself.
13. I can be angry with someone I love.
14. I can take care of myself, no matter what circumstances I am in.
15. I do not have to be fully healed to be fully worthwhile.
16. I do not have to be perfect to be perfectly happy.
17. I do not have to be perfect, period. NO ONE ELSE IS!

Genesis Stage

The genesis stage is different for each person, but it generally involves a new openness to the spiritual aspects of your life. Those ACAs who gained comfort from a higher power early in recovery find that their spirituality blossoms and takes on new depth during the genesis stage. Those who have been scared or offended by the thought of spirituality are often chagrined to find themselves acknowledging—and valuing—their spiritual impulses for the first time. Once you begin to accept your spiritual impulses as legitimate feelings, your relationship to the universe changes forever.

Spirituality refers to the relationship we *feel* to the universe as a whole, while philosophy refers to the relationship we *think* we have to the universe. Spirituality goes well beyond the intellect by involving our emotions as well. As healing proceeds, your relationship to the world about you undergoes radical shifts. These shifts are particularly profound as your true self emerges, strengthens, and begins to eclipse the false self. You experience these shifts as changes in your identity. The subjective experience of coming into a radically different relationship with the world around you is deeply moving. "Spiritual experience" is probably the best label we have for such feelings.

The genesis stage emerges only after you have spent time living entirely within the scope of what is legitimately under your control rather than squandering energy on the uncontrollable. When you're fully aware of what you can affect in your life, you begin to move with new power. Concentrated and focused power, applied properly, allows you to become an actor, not just a reactor. In the genesis stage you begin to participate in the creation of your own world, not grandiosely but realistically. Genesis is the true beginning of your own unique life, with your own unique relationship to the rest of the universe.

The creation of the National Association for Children of Alcoholics (NACoA) is an example of the genesis stage operating on a large scale. Once you have accepted that nothing can change the realities that occurred during your childhood, you are eventually faced with the fact that there are children today for whom realities can be changed. By supporting NACoA's efforts to provide a voice on behalf of CoAs, your own healing can reach across generations. The next-best thing to being able to break your own isolation when you were young is to break the isolation of those who are young today. We can do this if enough of us begin to speak with one voice to young CoAs everywhere, letting them know they are not alone.

The creation of NACoA is described in conjunction with spirituality because its members believe that they are inti-

mately connected to one another. CoAs everywhere share a
common bond. The final stages of healing for each of us
involves acknowledging our relationship to the whole. We do
not heal alone. In the end, we are responsible for sustaining
the community that supported us earlier in our healing. This
is a way of returning the gifts that recovery has given us so
freely.

The subtle wisdom contained in self-help Twelve-Step
programs runs deep, because it embodies three vitalizing
actions: honesty, receiving feelings, and entering into community. When these actions are practiced in a disciplined way
until they have become a fundamental part of your life, they
are capable of unlocking the natural healing forces within
your mind and heart. Healing flows through channels that are
etched through the structure of your mind. Any efforts you
make to encourage your healing must move through these
channels; you cannot force growth along paths that do not
exist. A life committed to honesty, feelings, and community
allows your mind the most freedom to heal itself.

A commitment to honesty cleanses your mind of the
denial that contaminates your relationship with the world. It
is an article of faith for me that real healing does not begin
until your mind is focused on the realities affecting your life.
You cannot expect real healing to occur while you remain
identified with your false self. The first portions of this book
described the painstaking process of becoming more
grounded in the realities of your childhood, especially as
those realities continue to affect your adult life today. In a
similar way, the Twelve Steps begin by confronting your
denial about being a child of an alcoholic and then lead you
into the discipline of taking constant inventory of yourself.
When you work the steps, honesty becomes a deeply in-
grained way of life, and healing is promoted.

A commitment to receive your feelings—that is, to make
room for them—revitalizes the mind, the heart, and the soul.
Often, people believe they are in touch with feelings because

they are constantly spewing them out and acting on them as soon as they occur. A person for whom this has become a way of life is no more comfortable with his or her feelings than someone who is determined to keep feelings suppressed. In both cases, the goal is to get away from one's feelings as soon as possible. Receiving your feelings requires a willingness to experience them, to touch upon each facet of them, and to take the full measure of their depth. They can then move freely through your life without draining your energies.

A second article of faith with me is that the mind heals itself best when the realities of our feelings are not only acknowledged intellectually but are also experienced. It is strangely paradoxical that the more you try to control and disavow your feelings, the more you become prisoner to them. Like living, breathing entities, feelings behave differently depending on whether they are kept in confinement or allowed to move about freely. When your feelings are permitted to move freely within and through you, they take on different qualities and it becomes clearer that they have your best interests at heart. The false self imposes a master-servant relationship on feelings. This relationship can be relinquished in favor of a partnership, in which the natural healing forces of the mind can work most effectively.

A commitment to entering into community with others and with your Higher Power greatly speeds the mind's healing. Community brings a sense of belonging, of being a part of something larger, that can never be achieved in isolation. It is a third article of faith of mine that seeing yourself as part of a larger whole is invariably healing. Community adds a dimension and a purpose to your life that can never be generated wholly from within. Each of us is too small to create what community alone can bring into our lives. This book can provide you with only a hint of what community means. The next two chapters, on Twelve-Step self-help groups and therapy, examine the two main avenues available for actively developing a greater sense of community with others.

8.

A Time for Community: The Twelve-Step Programs

Today, for most ACAs, the road to recovery leads to one of the many Twelve-Step self-help programs that exist to guide ACAs, alcoholics, drug addicts, and their codependent families back to health.

The origin of current self-help programs is the fellowship of Alcoholics Anonymous, which codified the principles of recovery into a series of twelve steps in the mid-1930s. These steps became the backbone of a successful program of recovery that has gradually been recognized to be applicable to a variety of other similar problems. The first were those faced by people who are married to alcoholics (Al-Anon) and by their teenage children (Alateen). Now the programs also address drug abuse (Narcotics Anonymous and Cocaine Anonymous), eating disorders (Overeaters Anonymous), gambling disorders (Gamblers Anonymous), and compulsive spending (Debtors Anonymous). Recently, many adult children of alcoholics have also discovered the value of these same twelve steps, and they have been attending self-help meetings in rapidly increasing numbers (either through Al-Anon Adult Children of Alcoholics meetings or the newer ACA fellowships).

The Twelve-Step self-help programs work through two avenues: the discipline of working the Twelve Steps, and the personal fellowship of coming together in meetings of the recovering community. More than 3000 meetings for ACAs are held nationwide every week, in addition to the more than 23,000 weekly Al-Anon Family Groups. Virtually all urban-area phone directories contain listings for Al-Anon or AA, and a quick call will give you information about meetings in your local area.

A typical Twelve-Step meeting lasts between sixty and ninety minutes and usually takes place in rooms obtained at low cost in helpful hospitals, schools, and churches. Each meeting is usually attended by from fifteen to forty members, many of whom arrive a bit early to socialize. Chairs are often set up in a circle, sometimes around a table. There is seemingly no organization, except for a table with water for coffee and tea and another table for literature, until someone opens the meeting by asking everyone to join in the Serenity Prayer: "God, grant me the serenity to accept the things I cannot change, courage to change the things I can, and wisdom to know the difference."

The first meeting you attend will undoubtedly stir many strong feelings in you before you even arrive. It is immensely important to pay attention to these feelings. They will tell you a lot about your fears, your hopes and expectations, and your prejudgments about what you are about to experience. When you do arrive, your experience is likely to resemble that of Robert, who called my office ten days before Thanksgiving. Robert feared that his mother had started drinking again, and he was in turmoil about whether to go through with his plans to visit her for the holiday. He berated himself for still feeling afraid of his family at the age of twenty-nine.

I saw Robert twice before Thanksgiving. The first time, I could barely get a word in edgewise. Robert spoke with a pressure that had built up over years of frustration and silence. He blamed himself for an endless list of inadequacies: not being able to get his mother to stop drinking, not being able to stop caring about what happened to her, not being able to control his feelings. He apologized for *almost* crying in front of me. He constantly excused himself for imposing on what he called my "incredibly busy schedule." This was the first time he had ever sought any kind of help regarding his alcoholic family.

Robert said he dreaded spending time with his family because he always sensed a horrible tension in the air. No one ever acknowledged that anything was wrong, except when his mother was drunk. Then Robert's younger sister would get furiously angry, his father would get very defensive of the mother (while simultaneously complaining that no one understood how hard life was for him with a lush for a wife), and Robert would try to smooth everything over (except when his own sarcasm inevitably leaked out). The whole scene was so predictable that Robert could sense its approach. The pain of returning to all this was becoming more than he felt he could bear. He wanted out but saw no escape, which frightened him even further.

I told Robert that he needed to talk to some other people who were in exactly the same situation, and I suggested that he attend four meetings at one of the local Twelve-Step programs for ACAs during the next week. I told him that I would see him just before he was scheduled to leave for home, and we could make the final decision about the Thanksgiving visit at that point. The fact that there were others faced with similar difficulties seemed to come as a shock to Robert, as it often does for ACAs. However, he agreed to my plan out of desperation, though I could tell that he wasn't convinced it could change anything. I emphasized that I didn't care what he thought of the meetings. I only wanted him to concentrate on the feelings they stirred within him, both during the meetings and throughout the week.

When I next saw Robert, he entered the office with a sheepish grin and told me the following, with barely contained excitement:

When I went to my first meeting, I was surprised by how nervous I got. I wanted to turn around when I saw nearly a hundred people filling the room. I was enthralled by the fact that everyone there was the child of an alcoholic. They all looked perfectly normal and competent—well, at least *most* of them did. A few looked like they desperately needed help. Everyone was greeting each other like they had been friends for years. I felt like an outsider. They all knew what they were doing and what to expect from the meeting. I was the only one in the dark. So I just found a chair and tried to hide. But the person next to me said "Hello," and I blurted out that this was my first meeting. His face lit up, and he welcomed me.

The literature table was my initial refuge. Since I didn't know what I was supposed to do, I hid there until the last minute, browsing through the books and pamphlets. When I read a description of how ACAs are often intensely concerned with looking "normal," I realized that this was exactly what I was trying to do in occupying myself with reading material. I paid fifty cents for that pamphlet and took a seat. That's when the person in the next chair greeted me.

I was deeply affected, and very disturbed, by hearing the Serenity Prayer read in unison. All my antennae perked into the alert mode. It suddenly felt like I had walked into a cult. I became worried that this was more of a religious service than I had expected. So it was quite a relief when the secretary of the meeting said that the program identifies with no religious denomination.

Meetings traditionally follow the Serenity Prayer with the reading of a standard greeting, the Twelve Steps, and often a quick pass around the room in which everyone gives his or her first name. Many people are initially put off by the repetitious nature of how meetings open. There may be a sense that everyone is following some ritual by rote memory.

Eventually it becomes clear that the repetition at the opening
of each meeting is valuable. It continually orients newcomers,
who are valued for their tendency to revitalize the fellowship,
and it reminds members of the values the fellowship must
hold to remain healthy. Eventually, the repetition becomes a
source of familiarity, as each meeting becomes connected to
every other meeting you have attended.

Among the important values reiterated are the need to
maintain confidentiality (this is the reason only first names
are used); the need for each member to assess what portions
of the meeting have personal value (the suggestion that you
"take what you like, and leave the rest" is part of what is
repeated at each meeting); and the prohibition against giving
advice, criticizing, or analyzing one another ("There will be
no cross-talk" is also heard at each meeting).

There may be a few announcements about upcoming
events, the need to keep the coffee table neater, or the date
of the next business meeting. A telephone list may circulate.
Anyone who is willing to take a call during the week from
another member to discuss the program writes his or her first
name and phone number on a sheet of paper that is passed
around. Many people simply pass the list on without looking
at it. Everyone is welcome to copy down names and numbers.
The list is a powerful tool of recovery for many people, since
it means they are never more than a phone call away from a
mini-meeting.

Another first impression newcomers invariably have
stems from the tradition of having those at meetings introduce
themselves by their first names (often following this by saying
that they are ACAs). The entire group then greets each person
by saying "Hi" and repeating the person's name. This affects
almost everyone who experiences it for the first time. Some
are overwhelmed by the thought of having that many people
focusing attention on them; others are attracted to the thought
of having their presence validated by having everyone greet
them; and some feel ready to walk out because all this seems

too cultish to them. If this tradition bothers you, ignore it. Concentrate on the parts of the meeting you find valuable, and "leave the rest."

The reading of the Twelve Steps usually involves the secretary's asking one or more people to read the Steps in sequence. These twelve goals form the core of your recovery program. Their power comes from a subtle wisdom that is rarely apparent the first time you encounter them. It is a wisdom that taps into the natural processes of healing contained within our minds, deepening the channels so that the healing forces can flow through more freely. It is unlikely that the authors of these Steps understood the psychological sophistication that lies hidden beneath the simple language they used. They had less interest in psychological sophistication than in recording accurately what their experience had taught them. Only recently has their wisdom been appreciated throughout the chemical-dependence field, but few outside the field have taken these principles seriously enough to perceive their benefit.

Although the Twelve Steps are usually attributed to Bill Wilson and other founders of Alcoholics Anonymous, their origin goes much further back in time.* In recording the Twelve Steps, Wilson relied on many of the precepts of the Oxford Group, a spiritual movement active shortly after the turn of the century. The group's members were attempting to return to the purity of primitive Christianity. Their "Five Procedures"—to give in to God, to listen to God's direction, to check guidance, to make restitution, and to share—reflect a uniquely American brand of theology. A form of evangelical pietism, it amounted to a belief that salvation comes from outside oneself as a gift (pietism), and that this "good news" should be joyfully proclaimed (evangelism).

---

*A full treatment of the origins of AA and the Twelve Steps can be found in *Not-God: A History of Alcoholics Anonymous,* by Ernest Kurtz (Center City, MN: Hazelden, 1979).

Through the study and practice of the Oxford Group's procedures, alcoholics such as Bill Wilson and Dr. Bob, the original members of AA, began finding sobriety. As Alcoholics Anonymous coalesced, the founders tried to clarify the simple steps they believed had freed them from the tyranny of their obsession with alcohol. The core of this recovery was the freedom and relief that came from accepting the reality that their control over the world was limited. The Twelve Steps they developed are a condensation of wisdom from across the ages, tailored to lives that have been disrupted by obsession with alcohol.

The Twelve Steps of Alcoholics Anonymous

1. We admitted we were powerless over alcohol—that our lives had become unmanageable.
2. Came to believe that a Power greater than ourselves could restore us to sanity.
3. Made a decision to turn our will and our lives over to the care of God *as we understood Him.*
4. Made a searching and fearless moral inventory of ourselves.
5. Admitted to God, to ourselves and to another human being the exact nature of our wrongs.
6. Were entirely ready to have God remove all these defects of character.
7. Humbly asked Him to remove our shortcomings.
8. Made a list of all persons we had harmed and became willing to make amends to them all.
9. Made direct amends to such people wherever possible except when to do so would injure them or others.
10. Continued to take personal inventory and when we were wrong, promptly admitted it.

11. Sought through prayer and meditation to improve our conscious contact with God *as we understood Him,* praying only for knowledge of His will for us and the power to carry that out.
12. Having had a spiritual awakening as the result of these Steps, we tried to carry this message to others, and to practice these principles in all our affairs.

It is important that these Steps are seen as suggestions. If they are irrelevant to you at first but you find the fellowship of meeting with other ACAs to be of value, then by all means put the Twelve Steps on the back burner for now. Whether you begin ''working the steps'' or not, remember the promise (the ''good news'') that they hold. For virtually everyone who takes the time to ponder them, the Twelve Steps will reveal their meaning a little at a time. Sometimes they must be turned over and over in your mind for years, even decades, before their value is fully apparent.

The reference to God in the steps scares many people. ACAs often have a stunted image of God. Since the initial picture of God you develop comes from an expansion of what you see in your parents, this is not always very comforting to CoAs. In addition, many ACAs remember having prayed long ago to God for help, with no results. The drinking continued, so it seemed that God had ''failed'' them. For these reasons, the suggestion to ACAs that they give their will and their life over to God is often not very welcome.

It is important to note that the Steps state explicitly that you are to use *your own* understanding of God. The Twelve-Step programs are mute when it comes to what that understanding should be. Most people substitute the term *Higher Power* for the word *God.* The Steps are clearly not intended to turn you into a religious convert. They are simply encouraging you to consider that something—whether it is a spiritual entity, the group of people who have gathered for this meeting, or even your unconscious—is capable of giving you the valuable guidance that is unavailable to you when you are feeling completely alone and isolated. Again, if you continue to have difficulty with these ideas, put them on the back burner and forget them for now. Do not let them interfere with the value of meeting for the first time with other ACAs in recovery.

After the reading of the opening and the Twelve Steps, meetings generally are turned over to a single speaker (this is a different person each week). Up until that point, the secretary has run the meeting. The position of secretary rotates; usually, no one serves in this position for more than six months. While it is considered to be an honor to be asked to serve, it is only temporarily useful to a person's recovery to chair the meetings.

Speakers are expected to follow a formula as they tell their story. They share their experience, their strength, and their hope. You will listen to a monologue by the speaker for about fifteen minutes. Speakers talk honestly about the problems they have created for themselves in the past, usually by trying to control the uncontrollable; about how the Twelve Steps have helped them to resolve some of these problems; and about their current struggles to bring the lessons of the steps more fully into their daily lives. The emphasis is continuously focused on the speaker's experience, not on the misdeeds of others.

Following the main speaker's "share," other people have an opportunity to speak briefly if they wish. At all times the focus at meetings is placed on yourself, and not on the alcoholic or on seeking advice for solving problems. Many people are amazed and appalled to discover how hard this is after so many years of being focused on others. Robert described hearing the main speaker at his first meeting as follows:

> I have to be honest about how hokey the meeting looked at the beginning. I mean, I thought I had stumbled into

a cult. Everything was so structured when they read the opening paragraphs and people all said "Hi" to each other in unison whenever anyone spoke. The Twelve Steps seemed interesting, but they went by too fast for me to understand and contained a little too much God stuff for me to be comfortable.

Then the main speaker began and I felt riveted to my seat. The story she told could have been mine. It was the perfect first meeting for me. Everything I had thought was unique about my family suddenly looked more average. We are all behaving like millions of other people in the same situation. But what I was most impressed by was the honesty of the speaker. After describing herself as a child in an alcoholic family, she talked about her own feelings and how she constantly tries to smother them. I *knew* what she was describing. I never thought anyone else would be able to understand what I was going through—and here was this woman voluntarily sitting in front of a hundred people and completely describing it. For the first time, I thought I might not be crazy.

Speakers often end their share by suggesting a topic and then opening the meeting. For the next twenty to thirty minutes, members of the group who wish to speak take a few minutes to comment on how the speaker has affected them, on how the topic relates to them, or just to share whatever is current in their lives. Throughout the stream of brief shares, the focus is kept on yourself, your feelings, and how the steps are useful for guiding your life.

Again Robert:

Of course, the topic the speaker chose was perfect. She suggested we talk about resentments during the holidays. The whole meeting groaned. I didn't understand why until the next person spoke. He said he had come to the meeting wanting to talk about how horrible it is to visit home for Thanksgiving, but the topic reminded him that his own recovery depends on focusing on himself and not on others. I was just blown away during the next twenty minutes when one person after another spoke with such openness about the struggle to free themselves from their families. I began feeling such anger at my family that I lost track of what was said during the last part of the meeting. All I know is that I saw how consumed I can be by my own anger.

It is common for ACAs to become lost in feelings during their initial meetings. In Robert's case, the upwelling anger kept him from being able to concentrate on the shares that followed the speaker. He remembered the intensity of feeling that filled the room and some of what was said:

Liz: I was setting myself up to be lonely this Thanksgiving. I had not let any of my friends know that I wasn't going home this year, and so I was left with no one to have dinner with. When I started feeling sorry for myself, I remembered the program phrase that "No situation is so bad that I cannot do something to make it better." So I used the phone list for the first time, which turned out to be a real gift to myself. I've been using it almost every day since, and three of us are getting together to celebrate the holiday. I'll probably never understand why I have to get so low before I'm finally willing to ask for help.

David: I'm excited by something I saw in myself this last week, even though it is painful to see it. I had thought I was finished with the First Step until a friend mentioned the idea of "emotional intent." I immediately understood how frequently my emotional intent is to control my wife no matter how much I make it look like she is getting her way. I was about to say I supported her for allowing our baby to cry for a few minutes before we picked her up, when I realized that my real purpose was to get her to feel good about herself. When will I learn that I can never do that *for* her? All I can do is let her know what I'm thinking and feeling—and let her do with it what she will. I keep being reminded that the First Step has to be taken on more and more subtle levels. There is no perfection in recovery, just progress.

Helen: I don't understand all this stuff about recovery. Every time I come to these meetings, all I do is cry. Will it ever stop?

Robert said that when Helen began crying, the person sitting next to her reached over and touched her arm. The secretary reminded everyone that sometimes the only thing that can be done is to "keep coming back" in the blind faith that "it works."

Martin: I know how you feel, Helen. I couldn't talk for the first three months I came to meetings. All I can say is that it gradually changed when I became more open to my Higher Power. It helped me to focus on the Second and Third Steps before I could face how powerless I really am to change some things in my life—like how much sadness I have inside.

Shirley: I'm Shirley, and I'm a grateful ACA. I never thought I would say that. It always sounded so dippy when I heard others say they are "grateful ACAs." But yesterday I saw how out of it my brother is. He has no idea what he is feeling most of the time, even when he's real irritable. When I suggested that he try coming to meetings, he just about bit my head off for thinking our dad is alcoholic. I know he's feeling real miserable and doesn't have any place like these meetings to come to for support. So I guess I'm grateful to know that I'm an

ACA, and that meetings like this exist to help me deal with my life better.

At the end of meetings, time is often set aside for newcomers to speak or ask questions. No demands are made on you if you wish to remain silent. There is also a passing of the basket for donations. Self-help meetings have no fees. They are supported entirely by voluntary contributions; however, for newcomers the first meeting is a gift, and no donations are asked of them. Robert tells how he responded to his first meeting:

When the time came at the end of the meeting for any newcomers to share their feelings and experiences if they wanted to, I felt so touched by all those people taking the time to welcome us newcomers to their meeting that I raised my hand. When I was called on, I surprised myself by saying, "My name is Robert, and I'm an adult child of an alcoholic." I was overwhelmed by hearing everyone say "Hi, Robert" back to me. Hearing my name choked me up. I couldn't talk at first; they just waited. Finally, all I could say was that I needed to hear my name said by everyone to help make all of this real. The speaker thanked me and said that he hoped I would try six different meetings in order to see the variety of what is available.

The meeting ended with everyone standing, holding hands, and reciting the Lord's Prayer. The final words, spoken in unison as people continued to hold hands, were "Keep coming back—it works." As the prayer was being spoken, Robert found himself looking around the circle. The stories he had heard during the past hour contained so many of the threads running through his own life that he already felt he could trust these people. By empathizing with their fates, he had begun to feel a new acceptance for his own history.

The other three meetings Robert attended helped him begin to focus on his own role in the family. When I asked him if he felt he had a choice as to whether or not to go home for Thanksgiving, depending on what was healthiest for him, he admitted that he did not yet feel he had such a choice. He was still hostage to the family to a degree. But, he now knew that he could leave the house and go to a Twelve-Step meeting if things began to get too crazy at home. He no longer felt isolated in his problem.

TWELVE STEPS AND TWELVE TRADITIONS: THE DISCIPLINE OF RECOVERY

In addition to the fellowship of other recovering ACAs, self-help programs work through the Twelve Steps. When these are studied and put into practice, they help ACAs move beyond the reidentification stage to the stages of core issues, integration, and genesis. Before looking more closely at these later stages of recovery, it is useful to understand better how each of the Steps works.

1. We admitted we were powerless over alcohol—that our lives had become unmanageable.

The **First Step** calls upon you as an ACA to acknowledge both that you are powerless over alcohol and that your life has become unmanageable. How is this Step to be understood? If alcoholics are powerless over the effects of alcohol on their minds and bodies, then, by extension, their children are also powerless over how alcohol is affecting their parents. The First Step calls upon you to accept this powerlessness, which is the same as accepting the reality that your parent is alcoholic. Denial ends when we confront the realities of our lives. When your parent is alcoholic, resisting this reality will accomplish nothing for you. It will only delay your own healing. The First Step suggests that you willingly take on the label "adult child of an alcoholic." This honesty with yourself and the world opens the channels of healing that have been blocked.

Until CoAs accept the First Step, they continue to feel guilty that they were never clever enough or strong enough to get their parents to stop drinking. It never occurs to them that it is literally impossible to make another person stop drinking. It is possible to ask that they stop drinking, to suggest that they stop drinking, to refuse to be around them when they are drinking, to confront them with the damage they have done to their own lives and the lives of people who love them, and to invite them to spend some sober time with you. However, none of these approaches has the power to force them to stop drinking. Alcoholics have been taken over by the power of their disease, and you have no ability to change this fact.

If you continue resisting this Step, perhaps you should explore why it is so important to prove that you have such control. What is wrong with being merely human?

The first half of the First Step challenges your basic beliefs about your efforts to control an alcoholic parent. The second half offers the same challenge to your efforts to control the rest of your life. The reason you cannot keep parts of your life under control is not because you are inadequate but because those parts of your life lie outside the ability of any human being in your circumstances to control.

Children in alcoholic homes come to believe that life should be far more under control than what is realistically possible. They usually feel uncomfortable whenever they are confronted with parts of life they are not able to control. The recovery process for them involves a willingness to explore how these coping strategies have contributed more to the problems in their lives than to solutions. The First Step is just a suggestion, but the discipline of recovery is unwavering in making this the first suggestion you must face. Its position at the beginning of the list is a reflection of how the human mind works.

2. [We] came to believe that a power greater than ourselves could restore us to sanity.

3. [We] made a decision to turn our will and our lives over to the care of God *as we understood Him*.

If the First Step is difficult, the next two are no easier. They suggest that it is a kind of insanity to assume that your mind is the pinnacle of creation and that it must stand alone against the stresses of the world. The **Second** and **Third Steps** are based on the belief that you must rely on forces other than your conscious mind if you are to heal. The Second Step suggests that we are not alone; the Third Step suggests that we act on the basis of this belief.

The Third Step requires a leap of faith. It says, "You haven't done so well by following your own will. Why not try following what you believe forces greater than yourself might will for you?" For some this means following the will of the self-help group to "keep coming back." For others it means following the will of the unconscious to permit emotions to be received more fully. For still others it means facing God and saying, "Thy will be done, not mine." These are all versions of the same thing—getting out of the narrow confines of the false self you developed as a child.

The leap of faith contained in the Second and Third Steps creates a new sense of belonging and a greater accep- tance of your feelings. The single most effective way to recap- ture your capacity to belong is through the willingness to take a leap of faith toward God. Communion with God, however you might conceive such a Higher Power to exist, reopens the capacity to belong and to feel at home—two feelings that CoAs lose touch with at an early age. The capacity to belong affects our relationships with both the outside and inside worlds. It permits us to enter into friendships and feel wel- come, and it also allows us to enter a new relationship with our own emotions.

4. [We] made a searching and fearless moral inventory of ourselves.

5. [We] admitted to God, to ourselves and to another human being the exact nature of our wrongs.

The **Fourth Step** is an exercise in objectivity about yourself. You are asked to write down a thorough inventory of your strengths and liabilities, your virtues and your foibles, past and present. The **Fifth Step** suggests that this inventory is completed only by sharing it with someone else in the program who you feel is further along in recovery than you are. The ultimate goal is to stand before your God and speak the truth about yourself as best you know it, without dramatizing your shortcomings or understating your virtues. These two steps require rigid honesty, particularly when it comes to evaluating our virtues, since most of us are convinced that we will recover faster if we give special emphasis to the harm we have done to others. Such emphasis is a form of manipulation by which we attempt to impress our Higher Power.

6. [We] were entirely ready to have God remove all these defects of character.

7. [We] humbly asked Him to remove our shortcomings.

The **Sixth Step** suggests that we become "entirely ready" to have God remove all our defects of character. I don't know about you, but I'm not sure who I would be without my character defects—my pettiness, irritability, resentments, self-centeredness, and willingness to neglect my relationship with God. Finding the readiness to be done with all of these things and giving up the secondary gains they bring me means taking a mammoth leap of faith. I suspect this is the moment when we become more attached to our true self than we are to our false self. Most of us are so attached to the external identity we have forged, so impressed by the complexity of our creation, that we find it very difficult to abandon it forever. As long as this is true, we have not yet become "entirely ready" to take the **Seventh Step** and ask God to remove our defects.

In taking any of these Steps, whenever we stand paralyzed by our fear of the unknown it is best to start again at the First Step. Doing so reminds us that we are powerless to erase our fear of the unknown. Such fear is normal, but we do not have to handle it alone. We can rely on our Higher Power to help us move through it. Refusal to rely on a Higher Power may be one of the defects of character on our inventory. Admitting this defect to ourselves, to another person, and to God will probably move us one step closer to being "entirely ready" to be free of it.

8. [We] made a list of all persons we had harmed and became willing to make amends to them all.

9. [We] made direct amends to such people wherever possible except when to do so would injure them or others.

10. [We] continued to take personal inventory and when we were wrong, promptly admitted it.

The next three steps continue the process of being rigidly honest about yourself, turning that honesty into a way of life and deepening your willingness to bring new levels of honesty into your current relationships. The **Eighth Step** suggests that we write down an inventory of harm we have caused other people, take the leap of faith that comes with being willing to face the consequences of our past actions, admit the damage we have done, apologize, and repair the damage where possible. The **Ninth Step** suggests that we act on this willingness and clean up our past. We may feel intense discomfort and embarrassment as we face the people to whom we must make amends. But the reward is freedom from our guilt.

Once the past has been dealt with honestly, you are ready for the **Tenth Step**, which is a commitment to keeping the slate clean. A backlog of guilt need never accumulate again if you continue to be honest about your actions and promptly acknowledge any harm that you do. The Tenth Step gives you a solid internal foundation upon which to base your self-esteem. Your willingness to deal honestly with yourself becomes the guiding standard for your life, and your own sense of integrity becomes more important than the impressions others have of you.

11. [We] sought through prayer and meditation to improve our conscious contact with God *as we understood Him,* praying only for knowledge of His will for us and the power to carry that out.

12. Having had a spiritual awakening as the result of these steps, we tried to carry this message to others, and to practice these principles in all our affairs.

The final two steps bring fullness to your spiritual life and thus to your healing. The **Eleventh Step** is a commitment to whatever spiritual disciplines improve your conscious contact with a Higher Power. Again, introspection is followed by action, as the **Twelfth Step** suggests that you carry the "good news" of the transformation in your life to others in need.

In addition to the Twelve Steps, self-help programs follow a critical set of Twelve Traditions. Familiarity with the Traditions and how they are put into practice is a valuable tool in assessing whether a particular meeting is likely to provide the health and safety you need for your own healing. Just as the Steps nurture the individual member's health, the

Traditions safeguard the group's health. They form the larger container, the structure that keeps all self-help meetings united in their purpose and form. This unity is of paramount importance, since personal progress for the greatest number depends upon it.

The Twelve Traditions of Al-Anon (Adapted from Alcoholics Anonymous)

1. Our common welfare should come first; personal progress for the greatest number depends on unity.
2. For our group purpose there is but one authority—a loving God as He may express Himself in our group conscience. Our leaders are but trusted servants; they do not govern.
3. The relatives of alcoholics, when gathered together for mutual aid, may call themselves an Al-Anon Family Group, provided that, as a group, they have no other affiliation. The only requirement for membership is that there be a problem of alcoholism in a relative or friend.
4. Each group should be autonomous, except in matters affecting another group or Al-Anon as a whole.
5. Each Al-Anon Family Group has but one purpose: to help families of alcoholics. We do this by practicing the Twelve Steps of AA *ourselves,* by encouraging and understanding our alcoholic relatives, and by welcoming and giving comfort to families of alcoholics.
6. Our Al-Anon Family Groups ought never endorse, finance, or lend our name to any outside enterprise, lest problems of money, property, and prestige divert us from our primary spiritual aim. Although a separate entity, we

should always cooperate with Alcoholics Anonymous.

7. Every group ought to be fully self-supporting, declining outside contributions.

8. Al-Anon Twelve-Step work should remain forever nonprofessional, but our service centers may employ special workers.

9. Our groups, as such, ought never be organized; but we may create service boards or committees directly responsible to those they serve.

10. The Al-Anon Family Groups have no opinion on outside issues; hence our name ought never be drawn into public controversy.

11. Our public relations policy is based on attraction rather than promotion; we need always maintain personal anonymity at the level of press, radio, TV, and films. We need guard with special care the anonymity of all AA members.

12. Anonymity is the spiritual foundation of all our Traditions, ever reminding us to place principles above personalities.

Most of the traditions exist to maintain safety and unity. A continuous turnover in leadership is encouraged to avoid allowing any individual to dominate the group. Decisions about group issues are always made by group conscience, with the only authority being a loving God, as each member understands Him, and the Twelve Traditions. Self-help fellowships never accept donations or amass property and wealth, lest this divert attention from the primary spiritual purpose. They have absolutely no affiliation with other groups and express no opinions on outside issues. Hence, self-help fellowships never enter into controversy. Within meetings, controversy is avoided by prohibiting cross-talk (that is, commenting on, questioning, or directing other members) and by placing the principles of the program above personalities. The prolonged airing of personal grievances is discouraged as unlikely to lead to a beneficial exchange of ideas, and thus the focus is kept on you.

Two Traditions deserve special emphasis and clarification. First, self-help fellowships are anonymous for two reasons. By using no last names and by reminding members to safeguard whatever they hear in a meeting, these fellowships create an important sense of safety. Beginners can thus be assured that they have a haven to come to and that their problems will not be complicated by becoming public knowledge. Anonymity is maintained for a second, less obvious, reason—to keep principles above personalities. By maintaining personal anonymity at the level of the public media, no individual member becomes identified with the program. This prevents damage to the fellowship by a member with a high public profile whose conduct may inadvertently reflect poorly on the program. Furthermore, it prevents individuals from being tempted to seek profit from their participation in the program.

Finally, there is the Tradition of working by attraction rather than by promotion. Much of the wisdom of Twelve-Step recovery programs lies in the recognition that personal freedom and integrity come from a rigorously accurate assessment of what we can potentially control and of what lies outside our abilities to influence directly. It is not within anyone's ability to control whether another person is willing to enter into recovery or not. The only way one person will ever be influenced by another's recovery is if he or she is hurting enough to search for new ways to live and to see that recovery has brought peace to someone else. The Tradition of working by attraction rather than promotion fully accepts that every human being is endowed with all the power needed to resist entering into the discipline of recovery.

CONCLUDING REMARK

It is important to repeat at the end of this chapter that there is no substitute for attending a Twelve-Step meeting. The experience is far more valuable than whatever intellectual understanding of the Twelve Steps that my words may have given you. Self-help programs must be lived to be fully understood. If you find yourself even faintly intrigued, I encourage you to explore this avenue of healing further.

9.

A Time for Courage:
Treatment for ACAs

For ACAs, self-help recovery programs can be powerful therapeutic forces. Sometimes they are not enough, however, and professional treatment is needed if healing is to take place. But as an ACA, how do you know when therapy would be of benefit? And if you do need therapy, how do you know whether the therapist you have chosen is qualified? Or how do you know what kind of therapy to seek?

These questions do not have simple answers that can be uniformly applied to everyone. Too much depends on the details of each individual's situation—especially in a world where treatment for ACAs is in its infancy. However, whether you are considering entering therapy or merely assessing the therapy you are already receiving, this chapter will provide useful guidelines in selecting the treatment that is right for you.

Remember, ACA is a label and not a diagnosis. The label is extremely valuable. It focuses attention on one of the major influences affecting your life. However, everyone seeks treatment for different reasons and with different needs. Be wary of therapists who think they know what you need simply because you are an ACA. Your treatment must be individualized.

Is Therapy Right for You?

The following list of questions may be helpful in determining whether you need more assistance in your recovery than Twelve-Step programs alone can provide:

1. Is your life threatened or your health in jeopardy?
2. Are you in a self-abusive relationship with alcohol or drugs?
3. Are intimate relationships still a problem?
4. Do you find yourself unwilling to attend Twelve-Step meetings?
5. Do you have difficulty enjoying the quality of life you have achieved?

1. Life-threatening situations can be either immediate or chronic. Your life is in immediate danger if you are thinking about suicide, obsessed with wanting to die, or becoming prone to accidents. Chronic threats to your life can also come from taking poor care of your health, subjecting yourself to excessive stress, or remaining in an abusive situation out of misplaced loyalty. The most common abusive situations ACAs find themselves in are being hostage to someone else's drinking or drug use or to someone's physical or sexual mistreatment of them. A therapist's help is usually required to overcome such deep-rooted patterns.

2. A classic problem for ACAs is overreliance on, or outright addiction to, alcohol and other drugs. Approximately 20 percent of the ACAs who come to me for therapy for "ACA issues" are in denial about their own chemical dependence. They need treatment, but not for their ACA issues first. That would be like trying to teach someone how to run a marathon while the person is still smoking. You need all of your resources and faculties operating at peak efficiency if you expect to make any significant changes in ACA problems. First things first: once the alcohol and drugs are out of your system and you are well into your recovery from chemical dependence, then you have a chance to begin making changes in how your past is continuing to affect your life. Some ACAs discover that other compulsions (such as eating, sex, work, and spending) can be as disruptive to recovery as active drinking. In these cases, too, the compulsive behavior must be treated directly in order for further treatment to become effective.

3. Sometimes it can be very difficult to change deeply embedded patterns of avoiding intimacy. ACAs can encounter insurmountable internal barriers to the natural healing forces. Your psychic numbing might be so deep that you have no memory of your childhood and of the traumas that led to your being the person you are today. Or, your codependence might be so pervasive that you cannot break free of destructive, abusive relationships. Or, your intimate relationships may be destroyed by your own abusive behavior toward others, especially toward your own children. No one wants to admit that yesterday's victim can be today's abuser, but this is often the pattern. If you even suspect yourself of emotionally, physically, or sexually abusing someone else, seek outside help immediately. You are almost certainly scared by and ashamed of what you are doing. And you almost certainly do not want the abuse to continue. Dealing directly with these issues in therapy can open you to the healing influence that comes from working the Twelve Steps.

4. If you are unwilling to expose yourself to Twelve-Step meetings, it is valuable to find a therapist who can help you explore why this is the case. I do not mean to imply that the Twelve-Step programs are a litmus test of health. However, coming to a realistic understanding of what you are recoiling from can be an extremely useful avenue for exploring your internal world.

5. Many ACAs spend a few years working with a therapist, not because it is necessary in order for them to be successful and happy but because it helps them to enjoy their success more fully. Their work with a therapist is similar to working with a trainer; it is one more important contributor to the quality of their lives.

A word of warning: It is important to recognize that ACAs are at high risk for a wide range of traditional psychological problems. Major depression, manic-depressive illness, and schizophrenia occur among children of alcoholics. Please do not fall into the trap of believing that working solely with your problems as an ACA will solve all of your psychological problems. The mental-health field has a long history of "overpromising" the power of every new therapy that is developed. This is largely because all of us—therapists and clients alike—hope that as much pain as possible can be relieved. Treatment for your ACA issues must be part of a larger, more encompassing approach to your health.

HOW TO CHOOSE A THERAPIST

Therapists are no different from any other professionals. They have entered into their work for a wide variety of reasons. The vast majority attempt to be as effective as possible and possess a basic sense of integrity. As with any profession, there are a few who stand head and shoulders above the rest, while the majority of therapists do very adequate work. However, a substantial minority are either too early in their careers, too late in their careers, inadequately trained, intellectually undisciplined, emotionally ill-equipped, or otherwise less than fully competent.

At times therapists have to educate. At times they have to support. And at times they have to challenge the past. The most effective therapists not only know the appropriate time for each of these kinds of therapy, but they also have a vision of what full health can be and will meet your immediate needs while preparing you to move on to the next stage of your healing. Certainly, *no* therapist, no matter how skilled, will meet all of your needs. However, since your recovery does not hinge on finding a therapist who meets all of your needs, your therapist needs only to provide substantial assistance to the natural healing forces within you.

The practice of psychotherapy inevitably involves a certain amount of guesswork. Therapists have few ways of confirming their conclusions. There are no X rays to back up their diagnoses, only experience, intuition, integrity, willingness to consult frequently with tough-minded colleagues, and ultimately, of course, whether or not you respond to the treatment they provide. The best therapists become comfortable with ambiguity and paradox (which is one thing that makes dealing with them so maddening and so intriguing at the same time). They are simultaneously confident of their perspective and open to questioning it at any moment.

It is very difficult to approach choosing a therapist with all the consumer skills you have for making major purchases, but this is the most effective attitude. As with choosing a doctor or lawyer, recommendations by friends or advisers are the best guides to finding a therapist who will meet your specific needs. I recommend beginning the search by obtaining at least two or three recommendations. It is often useful to ask many people for their opinion of who is the very best therapist in the community. Of course, such a person may already have all the clients he or she can handle but will probably be able to refer you to someone else equally trustworthy.

Once you have narrowed your list to two or three names, make an exploratory appointment with each. Prior to each exploratory visit, establish an understanding with the therapist that the appointment is merely to discover whether he or she seems right for you. Most therapists will be happy to respect such an approach. Do not make a decision until you have seen each therapist and have given yourself a couple of days to think it over.

There are three areas to evaluate when choosing your therapist: the therapist's training, his or her personal health, and the level of trust you believe you could develop in that therapist.

Training

At the moment, treatment for ACAs is dominated by people from the chemical-dependence field who recognize the special needs of children of alcoholics but do not possess all of the skills necessary for long-term treatment. However, now that therapists in the general mental-health field have become more aware of the treatment needs of ACAs, many therapists without previous experience in chemical dependence are also entering the field. As an ACA, one of your first considerations is to find someone with skills and training in both the general mental-health field *and* the chemical-dependence field. This is a rare combination, because there has traditionally been a gulf between these two fields.

As a rule, mental-health workers have not been adequately trained to treat chemical dependence, and so are generally very happy to have specialists to whom they can refer their alcoholic and drug-addicted clients. The chemical-dependence field is still so new that even today most training programs for mental-health professionals cover the issues of addiction in only a superficial way. As a result, most therapists are unfamiliar with the dynamics of recovery, which are of critical importance in any ACA's healing.

Chemical-dependence workers, on the other hand, do not need many of the skills needed by general mental-health workers. They can work quite effectively with the denial surrounding chemical abuse without having to deal therapeutically with early-childhood emotions. Their skills are those required for helping people in early recovery, where the focus is primarily on concrete ways to stay sober day by day.

Be sure to ask the therapists you interview about their experience in the chemical-dependence field, about their experience with long-term psychotherapy, and about their training in child development. After each appointment, ask yourself whether the therapist seemed to have large gaps in training or difficulty in answering all of your questions.

Personal Health of the Therapist

We all like to assume that every therapist has dealt adequately with his or her own personal problems. This is not always the case, however. A high percentage of therapists come from families that were unhealthy, often because of a parent's chemical dependence, and it is entirely possible that you will encounter a therapist who has not yet faced his or her own nature as an ACA. It is frightening how many therapists "discover" that they are ACAs and start conducting treatment groups before they have truly begun their own time to heal. It is even more frightening to see ACAs being treated by therapists who are unwilling to look at their own alcohol and drug usage. The world is a very imperfect place, and you would be well-advised to pay some attention to the personal health of the therapist you choose.

I believe it is important for a therapist to feel completely comfortable in working with alcoholics and drug abusers before he or she begins to treat ACAs. Any fear or distaste the therapist may feel toward people who are chemically dependent will contaminate the therapy and may simply reinforce the very attitudes you are struggling to overcome. It is very difficult to develop healthier attitudes than those of the therapist on whom you are relying. While this can happen, it is the role of the therapist to facilitate your growth, not to serve as a barrier.

Your Level of Trust

There is a temptation to believe that the therapist with whom you feel the most comfortable is the correct one for you. But comfort comes from many sources and is not as reliable as trust. You may feel comfortable because your therapist is in denial about the same things you are, or because the therapist is willing to take too much responsibility for your life rather than confronting you with the choices that only you can make for yourself, or because the therapist avoids feelings as much as you do. The goal of therapy is not to feel comfortable—it is to feel whatever it is that you are really feeling.

What you need in a therapist is a person you can trust and who will help you discover the truth about yourself. If you have ever been in the presence of someone who does not waste effort on facades and half-truths, you probably know the discomfort of being called upon to be more honest yourself. Look for a therapist who pursues honesty more than comfort. He or she will give you the opportunity to develop the rigid honesty that alone has the power to set you free from the past.

THE DIFFERENT VARIETIES OF INDIVIDUAL AND GROUP THERAPY

Another question that faces ACAs in search of outside help is, Which of the often bewildering variety of therapies will best meet their individual needs? Should you choose psychoanalysis? Behavior modification? Bioenergetic work? Talk therapy? Gestalt? Psychodrama? Workshops? Residential treatment? Group therapy? Individual therapy? Or one of the hundreds of other choices? It may feel a little like having a small inheritance to put into a mutual fund and suddenly having more than a thousand choices, all claiming to be the best.

The following brief guide to the major forms of treatment may help you to determine which is the most suitable for you.

Residential Treatment

Occasionally, an ACA reaches a crisis of such life-threatening proportions that inpatient treatment becomes a necessity. Or, an ACA may become so stalled in recovery that the intensity of a residential treatment program becomes a valuable tool, a catalyst to self-growth. In either case, there is now a growing number of residential programs for ACAs and codependents. These programs generally range in length from five days to four weeks. When people are brought into a residential setting, the entire milieu becomes the vehicle by which treatment is delivered. Through a combination of lectures, homework, journal writing, group therapy, and experiential exercises, an atmosphere of health and recovery is created. Not only are residential treatment centers a sanctuary and a respite from the conditions that created the crisis, but in addition their programs provide a vision of recovery capable of rekindling hope even in those who have become cynical or apathetic.

The shorter programs (lasting generally from five to eight days) tend to have a beginning, a middle, and an end. Everyone enters the program at the same time and moves through the treatment as part of a group. This structure is not designed to accommodate emergency care, since it does not permit you to enter halfway through a treatment cycle. The fact that everyone begins together permits a more powerful orchestration of the experience. Topics and exercises are often graded to build upon one another, with several emotional peaks followed by quiet time for assimilating what has just been experienced. The integrated nature of such programs often creates bonds of such intensity that lifelong friendships are created.

The longer programs (generally, four weeks in length) cycle continuously through a series of lectures, groups, and exercises in such a way that you can enter the program at any point. Treatment is individualized through readings, homework assignments, and one-on-one counseling. The value of entering a longer program is twofold. First, the longer length allows your strength to rebuild much more than it can during a shorter program. A longer program provides you with enough time to "detox" from the troubled living situations you may have spent years tolerating. You become completely immersed in your therapy, and you have time to make concrete plans for changing your living situation after you leave the program. Some things cannot be hurried, and a four-week program provides adequate time for reflection. Second, a longer program gives you the chance to make contact during your first days of treatment with people who have almost finished their stay. You can see the hope and strength that has grown within them during four short weeks. The possibility of your own healing becomes more real when you see it in others.

If you are considering residential treatment or workshops designed for ACAs, you should understand that the benefit from such experiences, for all their intensity, is often short-lived unless these experiences are part of an ongoing commitment to the discipline of recovery. The best residential treatment is always connected to ongoing therapy. It takes time to integrate the lessons and the emotions experienced during the intense phase of residential treatment. Do not expect miracles. Or perhaps I should say, do not expect miracles without a lot of work to nurture and sustain them.

Group Therapy

When conducted properly, group therapy is frequently the most effective treatment available. Since ACAs are so practiced at sensing very subtle cues from other people, you can probably tell very quickly what your individual therapist expects of you if you are going to be a good client (what ACA does not want to be a *very* good client—the best client the therapist has?). This can lead you to present a false self. The habit of becoming what other people want you to be breaks down in a group. Suddenly, the whole setting is less under your control. What you say may please some people but displease others. It becomes much more difficult to mold your actions and feelings to the needs of others because there are too many others to take into account.

Each style of group therapy—and there are many—has its distinct advantages and disadvantages. Unfortunately, therapists are not always as careful as they need to be in clarifying, even in their own minds, exactly which style of group they are conducting. As a result, different styles and techniques of group therapy are often mixed together, although each has been designed to achieve distinct goals. When this happens, groups become far less effective than they could be.

The public nature of group therapy, as opposed to the private and potentially more controllable nature of individual therapy, may cause you some anxiety and prove a difficult hurdle to cross. Two types of groups exist that are not actually therapy, but that may well serve as a bridge that will enable you to move comfortably into a more public setting. The first type is self-help groups. Although self-help meetings are not (and should not attempt to be, according to their own traditions) group therapy, they *are* public groups. A second type of group, also not intended to be group therapy, takes the form of the public lectures and educational series frequently offered by chemical-dependence treatment centers and local National Council of Alcoholism chapters. When I am seeing clients in individual therapy, I usually refer them to such public education, since I feel that not all of their educational needs can be met within therapy.

By attending a lecture series, you not only begin to shed the stigma of your family but you also find yourself sitting in a room with other CoAs. As you watch others react to the new information, you realize that your own reactions are not bizarre. You can begin to accept that you are suffering from normal reactions to an abnormal situation. And you may begin to see that nothing is so bad that it cannot be talked about openly. The silence has been broken by others, even if you are still having trouble breaking it yourself.

In addition to the self-help meetings and lectures, at least four types of therapy groups exist. Topic-oriented **discussion groups,** in which ACAs are led to express their thoughts and feelings, is the most common style of group therapy offered. Generally lasting anywhere from six to eighteen weeks, discussion groups are extremely valuable in several ways. When well designed, they provide an integrated, methodical introduction to information relevant to the understanding of ACA issues. They also provide sufficient time for group members to discuss and assimilate the information presented on each topic. Discussion groups move beyond the general information about ACAs presented in educational lectures (such as "Alcoholic families keep secrets") and concentrate on the specifics of your own life ("What are the secrets *your* family kept?"). They also deepen the bonds you feel with other ACAs, which further decreases the chronic sense of isolation that plagues so many ACAs. Finally, because most discussion groups are of limited duration, they provide an avenue for testing the therapeutic waters without making an open-ended commitment.

Less structured **support groups** are a second style of group therapy. Support groups are similar to discussion groups but tend to focus more on current events in the lives of the group members rather than on a course of topics. When topics are introduced, they are more general in nature (for example, assertiveness training, communication skills, or recovery planning). Support groups are more often open-ended; that is, there is no specific date set for disbanding the group. The discussion of current problems helps members to gain a better perspective on their lives and to develop alternative strategies for dealing effectively with their problems. The emphasis tends to be less on understanding the past and more on changing how the legacy of that past continues to affect the present.

A third style, called **experiential group therapy,** uses techniques such as guided imagery, psychodrama, Gestalt, body-movement exercises, and so on to unblock feelings. These techniques are particularly valuable when more verbally oriented therapies are unable to reach your emotions. They can be integrated into both discussion and support groups to bring feelings into the present moment, where they can be directly experienced.

However, the power and emotional intensity of experiential groups can obscure the fact that considerable work needs to be done if the insights and experiences they produce are going to lead to lasting change. Also, such groups can seem intrusive to ACAs suffering from PTSD or to those who are still too early in the healing process to access their feelings. Another problem with experiential groups is the risk of placing the therapist in too central a position. Group members rely on the leader to suggest, conduct, and control the exercises during each meeting, and sometimes a "guru mentality" can develop. In short, experiential groups offer higher gain than discussion and support groups, but at a higher risk on an emotional level.

Finally, there are **interactional groups,** which focus on the spontaneous events that occur during the meetings themselves. At times the focus will shift to past memories or to current life problems outside the group setting, but it is always guided back to the relationships that are developing, or failing to develop, among group members. In effect, the group sessions become a microcosm of your world. If you tend to put others' needs first in your outside life, you will also begin to put the needs of other group members first. If you tend to let people in your outside life get only so close before you put up a wall, you will put up the same wall as group members begin to get close to you. In the interactional group, the patterns in effect throughout your life are pointed out to you at the very moment they arise, and you hear honestly from others how they are really reacting to you. Deciding how you should have behaved two days after an event has a very different effect than being presented with the chance to behave differently right in the midst of the event itself. Interactional groups give you the opportunity to make different choices about your behavior when it most counts.

Interactional groups are generally long-term, with no definite date for ending. They are most effective if they are run by cotherapists, preferably a male/female team. They are also more effective if group members do not seek contact with one another between meetings or go into individual therapy with either of the group therapists. This is so that no group member will be relating to another "behind closed doors," where so many things get settled in alcoholic families. This guideline means that you will never be left wondering why two group members who were angry with each other in one meeting are acting like the best of friends at the next meeting. If things are going to get settled, they are going to get settled *in the group.* The more strictly this guideline can be followed, the more valuable the group becomes as a laboratory for studying your own behavior and a workbench for trying out new alternatives.

Individual Therapy

There is often a great deal of confusion about whether individual or group therapy is best. Some people seem to have the impression that group therapy is somehow second-rate—a way to provide more treatment to more people at less cost. The truth is that both are extremely powerful means of therapy, but they serve different goals. Neither can substitute for the other.

In individual therapy, the focus is wholly on you and on

the relationship between you and your therapist. This is crucial in dealing with intense anxiety or depression, psychic numbing, crises that demand concentrated help, severely disorganized thinking, and the excessive intellectualization that ACAs use to isolate themselves from their feelings.

In addition, individual therapy is a powerful tool for exploring the unfinished business that remains between you and your parents. There is a lot of attention given in the ACA field to "reparenting yourself." This entails treating the childlike parts of yourself with the respect and validation you wish you had been treated with by your parents when you were a child. The problem with reparenting yourself is that you have probably been parenting yourself in one way or another your whole life. Individual therapy offers you an opportunity to allow someone else to parent you, if only symbolically. In such a relationship, you can finish your end of the unfinished business with your parents and experience, on an emotional level, your own adequacy, both as an adult and as a child. This is the next best thing to being able to talk to your parents about your feelings toward them and have them listen to you. Achieving this "next best thing" is the goal of this kind of therapy. It can be a very powerful healing force in your life.

It can also be a profoundly embarrassing, confusing, and terrifying experience. Why would you tell anyone in a position of authority what you are really feeling, especially about them? Your past experiences tell you that this is insane. Since childhood, your goal has been to protect yourself from people in authority, not to make yourself more vulnerable to them. Therapists are fully aware that doing this requires a leap of faith on your part. They know that they cannot take this leap for you. All they can do is help you be honest about how much pain you create in your life when you keep your feelings buried, and help you to understand that you must either take that leap or remain stuck where you are.

The difference between your original relationship with your parents and your relationship with your therapist is that

this time your feelings do not have to be kept secret. They
can be expressed, sorted out, and validated. When your therapist continues to give you focused attention, no matter what
feelings you have toward him or her, you have an experience
you rarely had with your parent. You will find that this
relationship—and all your other relationships—gradually
becomes more vibrant and alive. You will find that you can
be exactly who you are without fear of being punished or
abandoned. This is the reward for your leap of faith.

Healing depends on this willingness to finish your own
end of the relationship with your parents. What they can or
cannot do with their end is totally irrelevant to your own
healing. That is one thing I can promise you without reser-
vation.

Karen is a thirty-seven-year-old writer who was in individual therapy with me for two years. At one point, toward
the end of her therapy, she looked at me and said, "You can't
do it for me any more than my parents could. You can't make
me feel good about myself, either."

I agreed and explained that it is natural for a child to
believe that parents are powerful enough to make the
child's life a success. Each of us must eventually grapple
with the fact that this is an illusion. In healthy families,
children discover this illusion very gradually, over the
course of a couple of decades or more. The truth comes
home to them only as they develop the maturity to deal with
it. Furthermore, their parents are comfortable with having
limits on how much they can do to make their children
happy. Eventually, as children from healthy families reach
their own adult years, they and their parents can acknowledge together the realities of being limited.

As I "reparented" Karen, the illusions that she had had
about her parents were transferred to me. She deeply believed
that I, as the therapist, had the power to make her happy. She
tried, in all the ways she had tried with her parents, to get
me to take over her life and make her feel at peace with

herself. However, I simply played the role that a sober parent should play. I gave her time to gain enough courage to relinquish the illusion on her own. I did not strip it from her. I did not take advantage of it. I did not explain things to her before she was ready to understand them. I did not disparage her for still having such illusions.

I simply nurtured her growth toward becoming an independent person as best I could, giving her the right combination of what she wanted and what she needed until the natural forces of healing within her had been released.

CONCLUSION

Entering therapy, like entering recovery itself, can be a frightening business. It means acknowledging to another human being that you have needs and that parts of your life are out of control. It also means that you have hope that another person can help you to find freedom and balance in your life. Trusting a therapist requires you to make an immense leap of faith.

The miracle is that we ever find the courage to take such a leap. When we do, we often find that our time to heal is finally at hand.

Afterword

In my imagination, I have met Huck Finn personally. I dreamed of being in the first grade and taking a class trip on the restored paddle wheeler *Delta Queen*. As I stood at the railing, watching the river slip by through the night, I was bothered by thoughts of how bad the drinking might be back home at that moment. A very old man pulled up a deck chair beside me and settled into it with a satisfied sigh. He asked what was on my mind, and I was shocked to hear myself tell him the truth. Perhaps it was the sense of peace emanating from him which unlocked the truth within me.

"Well, I've seen my share of that kind of trouble," he replied. "Ran away from it down this very river once. You running away too?"

"No, sir," I said in horror. "I'd never run away from home."

He gazed at the river. The moon's reflection off the water danced across his face, and I believed for a moment that I was watching the outlines of his thoughts pass through his mind.

"What happened?" I asked.

"Huh?" My question jerked him out of his reverie. "Oh, you mean what happened when I ran away. The first part of what happened got writ down in a book—mostly the adventures I had when I was still a kid. What happened after that would take a long time to tell. A long time. Let's just say that

I spent the rest of my life trying to make peace with the first part of my life."

"Did you find peace?" It seemed as if the questions he wanted me to ask were popping out of my mouth.

He mused silently. The shifting light on his face gradually took on distinct shapes, and I found myself staring directly at them without fearing his disapproval. The shapes grew into a parade of figures: an Indian girl and her father, the Teacher of the Medicine Wheel, cowboys, circus clowns, gold miners, city merchants, skid-road bums, Temperance Leaguers, preachers, an old black man, riverboat workers, and eagles—lots of eagles. But again and again the same tortured face of an angry man wove in and out of the changing mural. Somehow I knew that this face belonged to the man's father. Each time the visage appeared, the moonlight flickered brightly in the man's eyes and through his father's face. I suddenly noticed that I was crying.

"Where do those tears come from, son?" the man asked.

"I don't know, sir," I answered. "They were just all of a sudden there. I guess they kind of surprised me."

"Well, that's about the way I found peace. Seems more like it found me, though. You keep traveling down this river just they way you are, and it'll find you someday, too. I promise you."

With that he leaned forward and knocked his corncob pipe against the railing. The red glow of ashes flew through the dark and died upon the surface of the river. The man stood up stiffly and said, "Maybe I'll be able to tell you my whole story someday." Then he shuffled off.

"I'd like that," I called out. "By the way, what's your name, Mister?"

"Just call me Huck," he said, and disappeared around a corner.

As an adult, I have often thought about the images I saw moving across Huck's face that night. Were they a review of his life, or a preview of my own? Today I know that they were both, forged from the common bond that we shared and that all children of alcoholics share.

Huck taught me many things that night, and he became the first member of my recovering community. I felt the universality of my experience as an ACA in his presence. Not only did he help me to feel connected with other CoAs, he also put me in touch with my basic humanness. We all start our lives as little animals, passionate and bursting with life, sharing an absolute need to be deeply connected with other human beings. Because CoAs often have their aliveness ignored and their connectedness with other people broken, their fate clearly reflects what we are all made of.

It is a universal part of the human condition that we must heal wounds from our past. The illusion of perfect parents must eventually give way to the realities of who our parents are as concrete individuals. Their limitations invariably become our own, in one way or another, and their struggles with identity and self-esteem become the stumbling blocks that we find in our own lives. This is the human condition.

Children of alcoholics teach us about the very nature of being human. Their experience reminds us that self-esteem is not innate but rather comes from being valued by people who value themselves. And it reminds us that our sense of self emerges from the love that binds us to our parents and them to us. It is almost as though the real human organism is not the individual but the family as a whole. Life passes through us, from our parents to our children; when we die, the family endures. We think of ourselves as being independent and autonomous, but on a deeper level our lives are like drops of water in the river that is our family.

From children of alcoholics we learn that the discipline of recovery is a universal pathway. CoAs help us understand how to travel this path, and they prove that the rewards of recovery and growth are possible throughout life. Life deals us many things that are beyond our power to control, and CoAs teach us that inner peace depends on our willingness to accept this fact.

"To everything there is a season" means that our lives proceed by ebb and flow. We wish only to love our parents, but there is a time for hate as well. We wish only to dance, to laugh, and to keep silent, but there is also a time to mourn, to weep, and to speak. Only when we allow ourselves whatever feelings emerge from our hearts, without judgment or the need to act upon them immediately, are we blessed with the gift of healing. There is a time to suppress certain feelings and awarenesses that threaten to overwhelm us, and there is a time to allow these feelings to come forth again. When we allow ourselves the legitimacy of both these times, we find the balance and freedom that comes with recovery.

The most important gift Huck gave me that night was to help me see for the first time that my own father had a spark of the divine within him, as we all do. It was a part of himself with which my father never found comfort, and it remained largely obscured by his alcoholism. Unfortunately, he died before that spark was ever able to ignite and illuminate his life. I was never able to sustain contact with it, much to my sadness. But when I am open to fellowship with those who have found peace along the road to recovery, I feel as though I can briefly touch that spark again. And, because there is so much of my father in me, I can begin to sense my own spark as well. May we all let the spark that is within each of us guide us in our time of healing.

In this book I have tried to share with you my experience and understanding of the road to recovery. The time to heal is now in your hands, but it is not under your control. If you accept healing for whatever it brings, you will get the most value from it. But, if you concentrate on the ways in which it does not live up to your expectations, then you will receive less than what it has to offer. If you don't feel that anything is changing for you immediately, do not give up following the discipline of recovery. Allow your pursuit of honesty, acknowledgment of your feelings, and willingness to belong to the recovering community to continue. In this way you will plant enough fertile seeds that you can be assured a rich harvest will ultimately fill your life.

Appendix I.

If Your Parents Are Still Actively Drinking

If you are reading this section, you probably still care about what is happening to your parents. Their excessive drinking is probably a continuing source of pain, fear, anger, and loss for you. But you no longer need to feel caught in the middle. As this book has shown, you can nurture your own recovery, no matter what happens to your parents. There are also things you can do to impact your parents if they are ready to change.

It is important that you learn as much as you can about the disease of alcoholism. You need to become familiar with its progression as well as its signs and symptoms. This is your best protection against falling into the kind of denial that can do damage to you, your parents, and your family. Books such as *I'll Quit Tomorrow* and *Under the Influence* are helpful sources (see Suggested Readings). Educational lectures are offered to the public by many chemical-dependence treatment centers and by local chapters of the National Council on Alcoholism. Alcoholics Anonymous meetings are an excellent source of information about alcoholism and recovery.

No matter how severe the pressure to do so, do not participate in your parents' denial of the illness or in the denial of the effects that alcoholism is having on you and your family. For your own health, do not forsake the truth as you see it. If it becomes too painful to be around your family without joining in with their denial, you may need to temporarily limit or cease your contact with them.

Take control of what *is* under your control. Be certain that the contact you have with your parents is based on your own needs, feelings, and health. Do not let yourself get into situations where you cannot get away from them if you need to. Although it may be more expensive, rent a car when you go home for the holidays to avoid relying on rides from a drunk parent. If your parents visit you, set some boundaries, such as insisting that there be no drinking in your home or having your parents stay at a nearby hotel instead of with you. If your parents call you up when they are drunk, tell them to call back when they are sober. These actions may rock the boat and cause huge fights, but this trouble merely confirms the importance of maintaining your position. As long as your actively drinking parents cannot respect your boundaries, it is critical that you continue to enforce these rules clearly, consistently, and even inflexibly. It is because of their disease that you have to protect yourself in this manner. You are not doing it to hurt or embarrass them; you are doing it in order to continue having contact with them.

Attend Al-Anon meetings that are not focused only on adult children. By meeting other people who are confronting the same problem, you may find more support in dealing with an actively alcoholic family member. Al-Anon meetings also provide information about alcoholism, particularly the family aspects of the disease.

Explore whether the technique of intervention is appropriate. Vernon E. Johnson's *Intervention: How to Help Someone Who Doesn't Want Help* (see Suggested Reading) outlines how intervention works. Chemical-dependence treatment centers and the local chapter of the National Council on Alcoholism can recommend an intervention specialist in your area. If intervention feels right to you, it may save your parent's life. If you think intervention would not be successful because your parent is not ready for it, your family is not supportive of it, or your own recovery would not yet allow you to undertake the intervention without your feeling bitterness and anger, you will still benefit from exploring the possibility. Your willingness to do so becomes one more step on your own path toward healing.

You must remind yourself at every possible moment that you have not caused your parent's disease, that you cannot control it, and that you cannot cure it. If you are unable to accept these facts, surround yourself with people who do believe them.

Do not hide from the tears, the pain, the anger, and the embarrassment that you are experiencing. No matter how bad you feel, remember that you do not have to suffer alone.

Appendix II.

A Special Word to Friends and Relatives of ACAs

If you are reading this book because you are concerned about someone else who is an ACA, you may now be wondering how to use your new understanding. How can you help a friend, a spouse, a parent, or a child who is an ACA?

In the character of Tom Sawyer, Mark Twain has given us a warm picture of someone ACAs can trust and feel close to. Tom always respected Huck Finn for exactly who he was. He never tried to change Huck and never judged him. Instead, he invited Huck to become a part of the adventures he created. Tom was confident about who he was and thus allowed Huck enough room to be his friend.

The following list of "Do's and Don'ts" for friends and relatives of ACAs can be summarized in one sentence: "Take full responsibility for your own health, and accept that you have no more power to change an ACA than ACAs do to make their parents sober." If the ACA in your life is not ready for help, too scared to change, or not in enough pain to feel a need to change, you are in no position to make them feel otherwise. Acceptance of your own limitations to help is the most effective attitude to take.

Your help will be most effective if you approach ACAs with the following in mind. The "Don'ts" are listed first because it is important to begin by doing no harm.

215

1. *Don't* judge ACAs. In particular, avoid draw-
ing the conclusion that they are weak. In most
cases, you would be no different if you were in
their shoes. A little humility goes a long way
in preventing yourself from expressing judgmental opinions.

2. *Don't* try to control ACAs. They will either
resent it or acquiesce, and neither reaction is
helpful to their recovery. Furthermore, you
could not control them if you tried. If you find
yourself trying to force an ACA to be different,
even though you think it is in his or her best
interests for you to do so, you are working
against that person's recovery by entering into
a codependent relationship. I suggest that you
attend an Al-Anon Family Group meeting in
order to learn more about how to detach from
loved ones you are trying to control.

3. *Don't* take all the blame for others' problems
or assume all the responsibility for their feelings. Similarly, don't blame them for all your
problems or make them responsible for all
your feelings. It is important to be clear in your
own mind about what is under your control and
what is under their control.

4. *Don't* pity ACAs. This is demeaning. Having
empathy is more difficult than pity, but it is
necessary if you are to be of any help.

5. *Don't* become codependent yourself. Don't
base your happiness, your identity, or your
recovery on anyone else!

6. *Don't* let yourself become the only source of
support and help for the ACA. You can never
give the ACA everything he or she needs. If
you try, your relationship will suffer and may
eventually be destroyed.

7. *Don't* cooperate with the ACA's denial. At times a friend should make waves by refusing to share in someone else's blindness.

The "Do's" range from general recommendations for your own life to specific actions you can take with regard to the ACAs in your life.

1. *Do* take responsibility for your own health, and pursue your own recovery, if you are bothered by codependence or compulsions (for example, eating, work, sex, religion, or spending) or if you have the slightest concern about your own alcohol or drug use. The most effective gift you can give an ACA is the model of your own recovery. But this must be done for you— trying to work a recovery program for the sole purpose of teaching an ACA how to do the same is often a subtle form of manipulation and control.

2. *Do* assume that there are good reasons why ACAs are the way they are, and respect these reasons. You do not have to know the details. It is also important that you let ACAs know that you believe that there were real wounds underneath their scars.

3. *Do* accept the reality of the ACA's feelings. You do not have to like these feelings, but do not challenge their existence.

4. *Do* play a lot. There is no reason to put enjoyment on hold just because some problems still exist.

5. *Do* most of your helping by invitation. Suggest that the ACA read this book or other literature about ACAs. Invite the ACA to attend a Twelve-Step meeting with you (but be sure to

go by yourself if he or she refuses). Ask the ACA to look more objectively at how drugs and alcohol might be affecting your relationship. Be sure that you do this inviting only when it does not compromise your own health; that is, don't subject yourself to repeated abuse if the ACA does not appreciate your invitations. Also, don't always expect a positive response. An invitation that obligates another person to respond in a particular way in order to reward you is a form of manipulation.

6. *Do* support the ACA's pursuit of the most effective outside help and support possible. Share information on self-help programs, therapy, and the message of hopefulness.

7. *Do* be honest about how the ACA's behavior affects you. It is important, for example, that you let the ACA know how you feel when he or she shrinks from intimacy. Open communication gives the ACA an opportunity to begin dealing with the reality that lies beneath the facade, and it promotes your own health as well.

8. Above all else, *do* let ACAs live their own lives, even the parts that are currently out of control. If they are not going to recover, you cannot make them. All you can do is speak honestly about your feelings. If remaining in a relationship with an unrecovering ACA is too painful and destructive to you, face the facts honestly. If this means temporarily or permanently leaving the relationship, then do it. It is a difficult choice, but it is no different from the choices that ACAs face with regard to their parents.

Finally, a special word should be added for those readers who are recovering alcoholics and drug addicts. I have often heard your deep concern and guilt over how your disease has affected your own children. It is particularly painful to watch your child continue to suffer long after you have found the joy and freedom of recovery. The guilt you feel may seem entirely natural, but it is unnecessary and destructive. As long as you approach your child out of guilt, you will be contributing to the view that chemical dependence is not really a disease— that you could have chosen not to be an alcoholic or drug addict. You can feel regret and empathy for your child, but your guilt will hinder rather than help your relationship.

The dilemma facing you as a recovering alcoholic is deeply ironic. You have come full circle and now know the agony that the other members of your family have experienced. Their only recourse was to attend Al-Anon and Alateen meetings to help them accept that they could not make you stop drinking. Now you are in a similar position with your child. You must take the Al-Anon First Step as seriously as your family took it. As the saying goes, "What goes around comes around." The model of your own recovery is the only effective gift you will ever be able to give your child. If you continue to indulge in your guilt, you are not taking optimum care of your recovery.

In the end, you must take your child's experience of being a CoA seriously, but you must not take responsibility for your child's recovery. You may find that you are the first person in an ACA's life who has ever taken his or her experience so seriously. This attitude alone may be the most important help you can provide.

Appendix III.

The National Association for Children of Alcoholics (NACoA)

On Valentine's Day in 1983, a small group of professionals working in the CoA field joined to create NACoA, a nonprofit association "founded on a spirit of unity, compassion, and deep concern for all those affected by alcoholism." It has been my privilege to serve first as NACoA president and later as chairperson of its board of directors. Our mission, which has been clearly stated from the beginning, is "to support and serve as a resource for CoAs of all ages and those who are in a position to help them." In the five years since NACoA was founded, we have developed into an increasingly effective voice on behalf of issues affecting CoAs. NACoA's role is to raise public awareness of CoAs and of the problems they face, to educate professionals and community leaders, and to advocate increased services.

By August 1987, NACoA had grown to include more than 6,000 members. Fifteen states have been incorporated as chapters, and other states are in the process of applying to become chapters. Each year NACoA delegates and members come together with members of the general public at a national convention to set the agenda for the future. At the first meeting of state delegates, held in February 1987, it was resolved that support and funding be provided to secure the following priorities:

- That training in the developmental and psychosocial needs of children of alcoholics and/or other drug abusers be established for educators, physicians, and alcohol counselors, as well as for members of the clergy and for workers in health and human services, the criminal-justice field, and child-care and social services, in the areas of identification, intervention, and referral.
- That all federal, state, and private-sector alcohol and drug programs be mandated to provide age-appropriate prevention, intervention, and treatment specifically designed for children of alcoholics and/or other drug abusers, regardless of whether the parent seeks treatment.
- That a coalition of persons from multidisciplinary fields be established to generate and disseminate a body of knowledge and principles to define effective standards in the areas of identification, intervention, and treatment for children of alcoholics and/or other drug abusers.
- That early identification, intervention programs, and support systems targeted at children of alcoholics and/or other drug abusers be implemented in every school, from preschool through college levels.

NACoA's activities to date include the creation of a clearinghouse for information about CoAs, publication of a quarterly newsletter, testimony before Congress, and the launching of our Elementary School Project. With funding from Metropolitan Life Foundation and the PEW Charitable Trusts, NACoA is sending a packet of materials about CoAs to every elementary school in the country. This packet includes an NACoA publication, *CoAs in the School Setting,* that is directed toward school counselors and teachers; a set of six posters directed toward CoAs (one for each grade); and copies of a comic book about emotional abuse and CoAs, developed by the National Committee for the Prevention of Child Abuse in cooperation with Marvel Comics.

Although a tremendous amount has been accomplished within the past five years, we have only begun to scratch the surface of what must be done. NACoA must build an organization strong enough to sustain its work for decades to come. After the initial excitement about the issue of CoAs has faded from the public eye, we need to ensure that NACoA will have developed enough support to continue speaking out for CoAs until concrete changes have occurred and the goals outlined in the NACoA Charter Statement have been met.

I invite you to become a member of NACoA and to make a contribution to help the association continue its important work. Write to: NACoA, 31582 Coast Hwy., Suite B, South Laguna, CA 92677–3044. Phone: (714) 499–3889.

Appendix IV.

Diagnostic Criteria for Codependence

A. Continued investment of self-esteem in the ability to control both oneself and others in the face of serious adverse consequences.

B. Assumption of responsibility for meeting others' needs to the exclusion of acknowledging one's own.

C. Anxiety and boundary distortions around intimacy and separation.

D. Enmeshment in relationships with personality disordered, chemically dependent, other codependent, and/or impulse disordered individuals.

E. Three or more of the following:

1. Excessive reliance on denial
2. Constriction of emotions (with or without dramatic outbursts)
3. Depression
4. Hypervigilance
5. Compulsions
6. Anxiety
7. Substance abuse
8. Has been (or is) the victim of recurrent physical or sexual abuse

9. Stress-related medical illnesses

10. Has remained in a primary relationship with an active substance abuser for at least two years without seeking outside help.

From *Diagnosing and Treating Co-dependence*, by Timmen L. Cermak, M.D. (published by Johnson Institute, Minneapolis).

Suggested Reading

The following books will help you explore further what it means to be a CoA.

General

Ackerman, R. J. *Children of Alcoholics: Bibliography and Resource Guide.* 2d ed. Indiana, Pa.: Addiction Research Publishing, 1985.

*Black, Claudia. *It Will Never Happen to Me.* Denver: Medical Administration Co., 1982.

*Brooks, Cathleen. *The Secret Everyone Knows.* San Diego: Kroc Foundation, 1981.

*Cermak, Timmen. *A Primer for Adult Children of Alcoholics.* Pompano Beach, Fla.: Health Communications, Inc., 1985.

————. *Diagnosing and Treating Codependency—A Guide for Professionals.* Minneapolis: Johnson Institute Books, 1986.

*————. *Evaluating and Treating ACAs—A Guide for Professionals.* Minneapolis: Johnson Institute Books, 1988.

*Gravitz, Herbert L., and Bowden, Julie D. *Recovery: A Guide for Children of Alcoholics.* New York: Simon and Schuster, 1987.

*Gravitz, Herbert. *Children of Alcoholics Handbook.* South Laguna, Calif.: The National Association for Children of Alcoholics, 1985.

*Available through the National Association for Children of Alcoholics Clearinghouse (31582 Coast Hwy., Suite B, South Laguna, CA 92677).

Leite, E., and Espeland, P. *Different Like Me: A Book for Teens Who Worry about Their Parents' Use of Alcohol/Drugs.* Minneapolis: Johnson Institute Books, 1987.

*Lerner, Rokelle. *Daily Affirmations,* Pompano Beach, Fla.: Health Communications, Inc., 1985.

O'Gorman, P., and Oliver-Diaz, P. *Breaking the Cycle of Addiction: A Parent's Guide to Raising Healthy Kids.* Pompano Beach, Fla.: Health Communications, Inc., 1987.

Subby, Robert. *Lost in the Shuffle: The Co-Dependent Reality.* Pompano Beach, Fla.: Health Communications, Inc., 1987.

*Wegscheider, S. *Another Chance: Hope and Health for the Alcoholic Family.* Palo Alto, Calif.: Science and Behavior Books, 1981.

*Woititz, Janet. *Adult Children of Alcoholics.* Pompano Beach, Fla.: Health Communications, Inc., 1983.

Twelve-Step Recovery

Julia H. *Letting Go with Love: Help for Those Who Love an Alcoholic/Addict Whether Practicing or Recovering.* Los Angeles: Jeremy P. Tarcher, Inc., 1987.

Rachel V. *Family Secrets: Life Stories of Adult Children of Alcoholics.* New York: Harper & Row, 1987.

The Twelve Steps for Adult Children. San Diego: Recovery Publications, 1987.

The Twelve Steps: A Way Out—A Working Guide for Adult Children of Alcoholic and Other Families. San Diego: Recovery Publications, 1987.

Workbooks

*Black, Claudia. *Repeat after Me: Workbook for Adult Children.* Denver: Medical Administration Co., 1985.

McConnell, Patty. *Adult Children of Alcoholics: A Workbook for Healing.* New York: Harper & Row, 1986.

Alcoholism

Johnson, Vernon E. *I'll Quit Tomorrow.* New York: Harper & Row, 1973. (Available through the Johnson Institute, 510 First Avenue N., Minneapolis, MN 55403.)

————. *Intervention: How to Help Someone Who Doesn't Want Help.* Minneapolis: Johnson Institute Books, 1986.

Milam, Dr. James R., and Ketcham, Katherine. *Under the Influence.* New York: Bantam Books, 1983.